I0423701

PRESIDENT'S MALARIA INITIATIVE

Ethiopia

Malaria Operational Plan FY 2016

TABLE OF CONTENTS

ABBREVIATIONS and ACRONYMS

ACT	Artemisinin-based combination therapy
AL	Artemether-lumefantrine
ANC	Antenatal care
API	Annual parasite incidence (malaria cases/1000 population)
APS	Annual Program Statements
CDC	Centers for Disease Control and Prevention
CNHDE	Center for National Health Development in Ethiopia
CQ	Chloroquine
CRMS	Continuous Result Monitoring System
DDT	Dichloro-diphenyl-trichloroethane
DHS	Demographic and Health Survey
EFETP	Ethiopian Field Epidemiology Training Program
EHNRI	Ethiopian Health and Nutrition Research Institute (newly named "EPHI")
EPHI	Ethiopian Public Health Institute (formerly known as "EHNRI")
ESR	Epidemic surveillance and response
EUV	End-use verification
FBO	Faith-based organization
FELTP	Field Epidemiology (and Laboratory) Training Program
FMHACA	Food, Medicine and Health Care Administration and Control Authority
FMOH	Ethiopian Federal Ministry of Health
FY	Fiscal year
GHI	Global Health Initiative
Global Fund	Global Fund to Fight AIDS, Tuberculosis and Malaria
GoE	Government of Ethiopia
G6PD	Glucose-6-phosphate dehydrogenase
FMOH	Federal Ministry of Health
HDA	Health development army
HDAMA	Health Development and Anti-Malaria Association
HEP	Health Extension Package (or Program)
HEW	Health extension worker
HMIS	Health management information system
HSDP	Health Sector Development Plan
HSS	Health systems strengthening
HSTP	Health Sector Transformation Plan
iCCM	Integrated community case management
IEC	Information, education, communication
IPTp	Intermittent preventive treatment for pregnant women
IRS	Indoor residual spraying
ITN	Insecticide-treated mosquito net
LCD	Local Capacity Development Projects
LLIN	Long-lasting insecticidal net
MCST	Malaria Control Support Team

M&E	Monitoring and evaluation
MIP	Malaria in pregnancy
MIS	Malaria Indicator Survey
MNCH	Maternal Neonatal and Child Health
MOP	Malaria Operational Plan
NFM	New Funding Model
NGO	Non-governmental organization
NMCP	National Malaria Control Program
NMSP	National Malaria Strategic Plan
NSP	National Strategic Plan (Same as NMSP)
ORHB	Oromia Regional Health Bureau
PCV	Peace Corps Volunteer
PEPFAR	President's Emergency Plan for AIDS Relief
PFSA	Pharmaceutical Funds Supply Agency
PHEM	Public Health Emergency Management
PMI	President's Malaria Initiative
PQ	Primaquine
RBM	Roll Back Malaria
RDT	Rapid diagnostic test
RHB	Regional Health Bureau
SBCC	Social and behavioral change communications
SNNPR	Southern Nation & Nationalities Peoples' Region
TFM	Transitional Funding Mechanism
UNICEF	United Nations Children's Fund
USAID	United States Agency for International Development
USG	United States Government
WHO	World Health Organization

I. EXECUTIVE SUMMARY

When it was launched in 2005, the goal of the President's Malaria Initiative (PMI) was to reduce malaria-related mortality by 50% across 15 high-burden countries in sub-Saharan Africa through a rapid scale-up of four proven and highly effective malaria prevention and treatment measures: insecticide-treated mosquito nets (ITNs); indoor residual spraying (IRS); accurate diagnosis and prompt treatment with artemisinin-based combination therapies (ACTs); and intermittent preventive treatment of pregnant women (IPTp). With the passage of the Tom Lantos and Henry J. Hyde Global Leadership against HIV/AIDS, Tuberculosis, and Malaria Act in 2008, PMI developed a U.S. Government Malaria Strategy for 2009–2014. This strategy included a long-term vision for malaria control in which sustained high coverage with malaria prevention and treatment interventions would progressively lead to malaria-free zones in Africa, with the ultimate goal of worldwide malaria eradication by 2040-2050. Consistent with this strategy and the increase in annual appropriations supporting PMI, four new sub-Saharan African countries and one regional program in the Greater Mekong Subregion of Southeast Asia were added in 2011. The contributions of PMI, together with those of other partners, have led to dramatic improvements in the coverage of malaria control interventions in PMI-supported countries, and all 15 original countries have documented substantial declines in all-cause mortality rates among children less than five years of age.

In 2015, PMI launched the next six-year strategy, setting forth a bold and ambitious goal and objectives. The PMI Strategy 2015-2020 takes into account the progress over the past decade and the new challenges that have arisen. Malaria prevention and control remains a major U.S. foreign assistance objective and PMI's Strategy fully aligns with the U.S. Government's vision of ending preventable child and maternal deaths and ending extreme poverty. It is also in line with the goals articulated in the RBM Partnership's second generation global malaria action plan, *Action and Investment to defeat Malaria (AIM) 2016-2030: for a Malaria-Free World* and WHO's updated *Global Technical Strategy: 2016-2030*. Under the PMI Strategy 2015-2020, the U.S. Government's goal is to work with PMI-supported countries and partners to further reduce malaria deaths and substantially decrease malaria morbidity, towards the long-term goal of elimination.

Ethiopia was selected as a PMI focus country in fiscal year (FY) 2008.

This FY 2016 Malaria Operational Plan presents a detailed implementation plan for Ethiopia, based on the strategies of PMI and the National Malaria Control Program (NMCP). It was developed in consultation with the Federal Ministry of Health (FMOH), NMCP, Oromia Regional Health Bureau (ORHB), and with the participation of national and international partners involved in malaria prevention and control in the country. The activities that PMI is proposing to support align with the National Malaria Control Strategic Plan (NMSP 2014-2020) and build on investments made by PMI and other partners to improve and expand malaria-related services, including the Global Fund to Fight AIDS, Tuberculosis, and Malaria (Global Fund) malaria grants. This document briefly reviews the current status of malaria control policies and interventions in Ethiopia, describes progress to date, identifies challenges and unmet needs to achieving the targets of the NMCP and PMI, and provides a description of activities that are planned with FY 2016 funding.

The proposed FY 2016 PMI budget for Ethiopia is $40 million. PMI will support the following intervention areas with these funds:

Insecticide-treated nets:

As per the NMSP 2014-2020, the FMOH anticipates a need for 29.6 million long-lasting insecticidal nets (LLINs) by 2015 to protect all Ethiopians living in areas with ongoing malaria transmission, which represents 60% of the total population. The Global Fund is contributing the majority of the LLINs with PMI supporting the remaining gap. PMI cumulatively procured over 16 million LLINs between FY 2008 and FY 2015. With FY 2015 funds, PMI plans to procure an additional 4.785 million LLINs for replacement after the NMCP's latest universal coverage campaign, which is planned to be completed in late 2015. With FY 2016 funds, PMI plans to procure an additional 4 million LLINs for distribution to high risk communities to replace lost nets and protect new households and new household members.

Indoor residual spraying:

The FMOH's NMSP aims to provide 100% IRS coverage as a key malaria prevention measure in areas where malaria burden is high and in highland fringe areas with the potential for malaria outbreaks. According to the NMSP's malaria stratification, which is based upon annual parasite incidence, about 17% of the population in the country will be targeted annually for IRS. PMI has been implementing IRS in Ethiopia since 2008 and has supported a comprehensive range of IRS-related activities, including targeting and enumeration of areas for IRS operations, improved logistical planning and support, environmental compliance monitoring, entomological surveillance, and technical assistance and operational support. The PMI IRS program protected between 1 million to 2.9 million people annually through FY 2014. In FY 2014, PMI sprayed 667,236 structures, protecting 1,647,099 people and trained 2,886 people to deliver IRS. With FY 2015 and FY 2016 funds, PMI will continue to support safe and effective IRS implementation within 26 high burden districts in the Oromia Region, in addition to continuing to provide limited IRS support to 34 graduated districts. With FY 2016 funds, PMI will target approximately 480,000 houses and 1.2 million people, and will consider strategically expanding implementation of community-based IRS.

Malaria in pregnancy (MIP):

The FMOH's NMSP does not support IPTp with sulfadoxine-pyrimethamine due to the relatively low intensity of malaria transmission in most of Ethiopia. Malaria in pregnancy in Ethiopia is addressed through improving prompt access to diagnostics and treatment, prioritization of LLIN use by pregnant women, and enhanced social and behavior change communication (SBCC) activities targeting pregnant women in high burden areas. With FY 2015 funds, PMI is providing pre-service training for midwives and health extension workers (HEWs) to improve malaria case management services for pregnant women. With FY 2016 funds, PMI will continue to strengthen malaria case management of pregnant women at both the facility and community levels.

Case management:

The NMSP aims for robust coverage of high quality diagnostic and treatment services universally, especially at public sector health facilities in rural areas in order to diagnose 100% of suspected malaria cases within 24 hours of fever, and treat all confirmed cases according to the national guidelines. Since the launch of PMI, a total of 3.2 million RDTs and 11.9 million ACT treatment doses have been procured. In addition, in collaboration with regional and district health offices, PMI has supported health worker training, mentoring and supervision for quality malaria diagnosis using microscopy, and the management of malaria at district-level health centers and community-level health posts through integrated community case management (iCCM). Based upon an analysis of existing and projected gaps in malaria case management services, PMI plans to procure 2.9 million RDTs and antimalarials including chloroquine, primaquine, and severe malaria drugs. Furthermore, PMI will continue to strengthen case management activities in the public and private sector with FY 2016 funds.

Health systems strengthening (HSS) and capacity building:

As outlined in the NMSP, substantial resources are needed to strengthen health systems and to provide capacity building for malaria control in Ethiopia. PMI has historically strengthened the health systems in Ethiopia through support to pharmaceutical management and logistics systems, including quantification of malaria commodities (through the micro-plan), strengthening routine malaria surveillance systems, and building the capacity of health staff through both pre-service and in-service training. Additionally, PMI has supported the training of Ethiopian Field Epidemiology Training Program (EFETP) residents in outbreak investigation and response. With FY 2016 funds, PMI will provide coordination support for ORHB as well as nationally, EFETP training, pre-service training of HEWs, and empowerment of Peace Corps volunteers and local non-governmental organization (NGO) for malaria prevention and control activities.

Social & behavior change communication (SBCC):
Highlighted in the NMSP is the need for SBCC activities to supplement malaria case management and prevention efforts, especially while working through HEWs and the volunteer rural Health Development Army network. With FY 2014 funds, PMI supported the development and implementation of SBCC activities including delivering communication materials through several partnering local and international NGOs, faith-based organizations, and Ethiopian academic institutions. In 2014, as a part of the USAID/Ethiopia Local Capacity Development program, PMI/Ethiopia initiated and supported two local organizations' community-based malaria SBCC activities that targeted school children and religious leaders. Based upon an analysis of existing and projected gaps in malaria SBCC systems and capacities, PMI will target FY 2016 funds for broad-based SBCC activities that focus on key areas, such as improving LLIN utilization and treatment seeking behavior. PMI's support will include SBCC content development and distribution, and continued school-based and faith-based community SBCC activities that promote malaria prevention and control.

Monitoring and evaluation (M&E):

According to the NMSP, high priority malaria M&E activities through 2020 include monitoring for resistance to antimalarial drugs and insecticides, routine vector monitoring, national household surveys such as the Malaria Indicator Survey (MIS), strengthening surveillance data management capacity, establishing 40 sentinel sites, monitoring LLIN durability, conducting annual program review meetings to examine malaria data, and bi-annual supportive supervision. PMI has historically provided substantial financial resources and technical assistance for many of these M&E activities, including support for Ethiopia's Public Health Emergency Management (PHEM) system, the MISs in 2007 and 2011, and ongoing support for the upcoming 2015 MIS. PMI's ongoing support to routine malaria surveillance aims to enhance reporting from rural health posts where half of all malaria morbidity is detected and treated, and to enable reporting of more complete RBM MERG indicators on a weekly basis. The annual micro-plan collects comprehensive malaria burden and commodities quantification data. With FY 2016 funds, PMI will continue to strengthen the PHEM system and epidemic reporting, support the national malaria micro-plan, and continue LLIN durability monitoring.

Operational research (OR):

Currently there are few ongoing operational research activities in Ethiopia, and the NMSP highlighted that funding for these activities is inadequate. Through FY 2014, PMI had provided support to Ethiopia for several operational research projects including assessments of glucose-6-phosphate dehydrogenase deficiency prevalence, and malaria serology studies exploring relationships between school-based children and community malaria prevalence by RDT and microscopy, and health facility-based surveillance. For FY 2015, PMI plans to support operational research projects concerning chloroquine preventive therapy for pregnant women with a history of *Plasmodium vivax* infections, administering primaquine radical cure for *P. vivax* in hospital settings, and a study to evaluate the effectiveness of the roll-out of single-dose primaquine to reduce *P. falciparum* transmission. PMI also provided core funding in 2015 for a multi-country operational research activity that will assess safety aspects of the current iCCM protocols in malaria RDT-negative children at rural health posts. With FY 2016 funds, PMI plans to evaluate the NMCP's plans to conduct reactive case detection in elimination districts.

II. STRATEGY

1. Introduction

When it was launched in 2005, the goal of the President's Malaria Initiative (PMI) was to reduce malaria-related mortality by 50% across 15 high-burden countries in sub-Saharan Africa through a rapid scale-up of four proven and highly effective malaria prevention and treatment measures: insecticide-treated mosquito nets (ITNs); indoor residual spraying (IRS); accurate diagnosis and prompt treatment with artemisinin-based combination therapies (ACTs); and intermittent preventive treatment of pregnant women (IPTp). With the passage of the Tom Lantos and Henry J. Hyde Global Leadership against HIV/AIDS, Tuberculosis, and Malaria Act in 2008, PMI developed a U.S. Government Malaria Strategy for 2009–2014. This strategy included a long-term vision for malaria control in which sustained high coverage with malaria prevention and treatment interventions would progressively lead to malaria-free zones in Africa, with the ultimate goal of worldwide malaria eradication by 2040-2050. Consistent with this strategy and the increase in annual appropriations supporting PMI, four new sub-Saharan African countries and one regional program in the Greater Mekong Subregion of Southeast Asia were added in 2011. The contributions of PMI, together with those of other partners, have led to dramatic improvements in the coverage of malaria control interventions in PMI-supported countries, and all 15 original countries have documented substantial declines in all-cause mortality rates among children less than five years of age.

In 2015, PMI launched the next six-year strategy, setting forth a bold and ambitious goal and objectives. The PMI Strategy 2015-2020 takes into account the progress over the past decade and the new challenges that have arisen. Malaria prevention and control remains a major U.S. foreign assistance objective and PMI's Strategy fully aligns with the U.S. Government's vision of ending preventable child and maternal deaths and ending extreme poverty. It is also in line with the goals articulated in the RBM Partnership's second generation global malaria action plan, *Action and Investment to defeat Malaria (AIM) 2016-2030: for a Malaria-Free World* and WHO's updated *Global Technical Strategy: 2016-2030*. Under the PMI Strategy 2015-2020, the U.S. Government's goal is to work with PMI-supported countries and partners to further reduce malaria deaths and substantially decrease malaria morbidity, towards the long-term goal of elimination.

Ethiopia was selected as a PMI focus country in fiscal year (FY) 2008, and annual funding allocations were provided for PMI-supported malaria control activities in Ethiopia for each consecutive year through FY 2015.

This FY 2016 Malaria Operational Plan (MOP) presents a detailed implementation plan for Ethiopia, based on the strategies of PMI and the National Malaria Control Program (NMCP) strategy, specifically, the Federal Ministry of Health's (FMOH) National Malaria Strategic Plan (NMSP) (2014-2020) that was finalized in August 2014 along with the FMOH's application to the Global Fund's New Funding Model (NFM) in June 2014. The FY 2016 MOP was developed in consultation with the FMOH and NMCP, and with the participation of national and international partners involved in malaria prevention and control in the country. PMI activities proposed in this MOP support the NMSP and build on earlier investments made by PMI and other partners to improve and expand malaria-related services, including the Global Fund to Fight AIDS, Tuberculosis, and Malaria (Global Fund) malaria grants. This document briefly reviews the current status of malaria control policies and interventions in Ethiopia, describes progress to date, identifies challenges and unmet needs to achieving the targets of the NMCP and PMI, and provides a description of activities that are planned with FY 2016 funding.

2. Malaria situation in Ethiopia

Malaria transmission: vector, parasite, and human host interactions

Anopheles arabiensis, a member of the *An. gambiae* complex, is the primary malaria vector in Ethiopia, with *An. funestus, An. pharoensis* and *An. nili* as secondary vectors. The sporozoite rate for *An. arabiensis* has been recorded to be as much as 5.4 percent. The host-seeking behavior of *An. arabiensis* varies, with the human blood index collected from different areas ranging between 7.7 percent and 100 percent. *An. funestus*, a mosquito that prefers to feed exclusively on humans, can be found along the swamps of the Baro and Awash rivers and shores of lakes in Tana in the North and the Rift Valley area. *An. pharoensis* is widely distributed in Ethiopia and has shown high levels of insecticide resistance, but its role in malaria transmission is unclear. *An. nili* can be an important vector for malaria, particularly in Gambela Regional State. Detailed information on the basic ecology and distribution of these vectors in Ethiopia is provided in the FY 2008 MOP. However, insecticide resistance among these vectors has become an important issue, with implications for vector control strategies.

Plasmodium falciparum and *P. vivax* are the major malaria parasites in Ethiopia, with several recent therapeutic efficacy trials documenting that ACTs and chloroquine continue to have adequate effectiveness for treating these pathogens, respectively. To date, there have been no major problems detected yet with emerging drug resistance, or with counterfeit or substandard antimalarial drugs in Ethiopia; however, constant vigilance is needed regarding these important issues that have adversely affected the malaria control programs of many other countries.

Typical human and mosquito behavior results in most malaria parasite transmission occurring indoors during nighttime hours within rural households within the lowlands, and in the middle elevations, and only occasionally in the highland fringe areas of Ethiopia greater than 2,000 meters above sea level. Malaria transmission may also sometimes occur outdoors during nighttime work or social activities, or may be associated with temporary overnight travel to other districts in malarious areas. Recent published and unpublished reports indicate an increased malaria incidence among migrant daily laborers in various parts of the country, most importantly in the northwest development corridors of the country bordering Sudan and South Sudan. Many Ethiopian communities have a "low" and "unstable" malaria transmission pattern that results in low host immunity and significant clinical malaria illness risk after malaria infections, increased tendency for rapid progression to severe malaria, and propensity for malaria epidemics affecting all age groups. The epidemiology of malaria in Ethiopia, therefore, contrasts with that of many other countries in Africa with high malaria transmission where malaria morbidity and mortality mainly affects young children.

Malaria transmission: seasonality, weather, geography, and climate

In Ethiopia, the interaction of mountainous terrain with variable winds, seasonal rains, and ambient temperatures creates diverse micro-climates. Ethiopian weather is also influenced by tropical Indian Ocean conditions and global weather patterns, including *El Niño* and *La Niña*. When a micro-climate creates local puddles, flooding conditions, and warm ambient temperatures that persist for several weeks within a malarious area with low population immunity, the resulting *Anopheles* mosquito proliferation may cause focal malaria transmission to accelerate, sometimes explosively. In Ethiopia, malaria is highly seasonal in many communities, but may have nearly constant transmission in other some areas; at the district level, malaria outpatient caseloads may vary several-fold from year to year in an "unstable" epidemic-prone transmission pattern. Peak malaria transmission occurs between September and December in most parts of Ethiopia, after the main rainy season from June to August. Certain areas experience a second "minor" malaria transmission period from April to June, following a short rainy season from February to March. January and July typically represent low malaria transmission seasons in most communities. Since peak malaria transmission often coincides with the planting and harvesting season, and the majority of malaria burden is among older children and working adults in rural agricultural areas, there is a heavy economic burden in Ethiopia. Although historically Ethiopia has been prone to periodic focal and widespread malaria epidemics, malaria epidemics have been largely absent since 2004, after the scale up of malaria control interventions.

Parasite prevalence, altitude strata and annual parasite incidence (API):

The 2007 Malaria Indicator Survey (MIS) indicated that parasite prevalence (as measured by microscopy) in Ethiopia was 0.7% and 0.3%, respectively, for *P. falciparum* and *P. vivax* below 2,000 meters altitude. The 2011 MIS indicated that 1.3% were positive for malaria using microscopy and 4.5% were positive for malaria using RDTs below 2,000 meters, with only 0.1% prevalence above 2,000 meters elevation. *Plasmodium falciparum* constituted 77% of infections detected below 2,000 meters elevation. The 2011 MIS demonstrated a remarkable demarcation of malaria risk at an altitude of 2,000 meters, with a13-fold higher malaria prevalence at lower altitudes compared to higher elevations. There was essentially no *P. falciparum* detected by microscopy among persons surveyed within households having measured elevations above 2,000 meters in the 2011 MIS.

In 2014, the FMOH updated the country's malaria risk strata based upon malaria API, calculated from recent routine surveillance data from more than 800 districts, with strata as shown and defined in Table 1. A malaria risk map from this API analysis is shown in Figure 1, showing areas with malaria transmission risk by API classified as High (>100 cases/1,000 population), Medium (5-99.9), Low (0.1-4.9), and Malaria-Free (~0). Areas with the highest malaria transmission risk as stratified by district API appear to be largely in the lowlands and midlands of the western border with South Sudan and Sudan, with additional high transmission areas in or near the Rift Valley, which extends from the southwest of the country to the northeast. Many densely populated highland areas were newly classified as malaria-free (API=0), including the capital city of Addis Ababa.

Table 1: Malaria risk stratification of districts and planned interventions based on annual parasite incidence, Ethiopia, 2014

Strata	API cases/1,000 population	Elevation (m)	Population		Districts		Interventions					
			Total	%	No.	%	LLIN	IRS	LC	Case Management	Surveillance	IEC/BCC
FREE	0	>= 2000m asl	33,639,639	40%	290	35%	-	-	-	X	X	X
LOW	>0 AND <5	< 2000m asl	11,153,499	13%	101	12%	X	X*	Wa	X	X	X
MODERATE	>=5 AND <100		28,410,564	34%	287	34%	X	-	Wa	X	X	X
HIGH	>=100		11,023,284	13%	157	19%	X	X	Wa	X	X	X
Grand Total			84,226,986	100%	835	100%						

*32% of low-risk population in highland fringe areas will be covered by IRS to ensure protection of this segment from anticipated epidemics. 68% of at risk population in low transmission will be covered by LLINs; WA: where applicable; LC: larval control; IEC/BCC: information education communication/behavior change communication (Data sources: PHEM and micro-planning 2013). (Note that PMI does not currently provide funding support for larvicidal activities in Ethiopia.)

Figure 1: Malaria risk map of districts by annual parasite incidence, Ethiopia, 2014

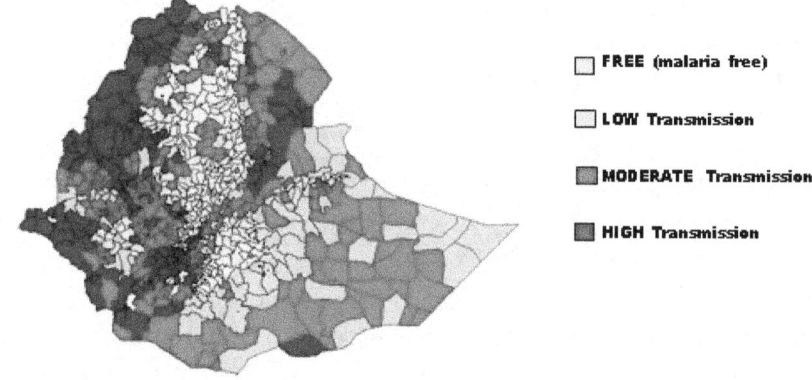

FREE (malaria free)

LOW Transmission

MODERATE Transmission

HIGH Transmission

Malaria surveillance systems and malaria trends:

Since 2004, Ethiopia's health systems for case management and surveillance have been greatly strengthened. There are three major overlapping and complementary Ethiopian health facility-based surveillance systems that provide information about malaria trends: the health management information system (HMIS) data, published in the annual Health and Health Related Indicator Report, the PHEM system data, published in the FMOH's Annual Review Meeting report, and the unpublished annual malaria commodity micro-planning survey of district health officers.

Between July 2013 and June 2014, the HMIS received malaria morbidity and mortality reports from 3,338 facilities (96%), out of the total public sector infrastructure of 156 hospitals and 3,335 health centers; this represents both a five-fold increase of health facilities and malaria reporting since 2004, and has facilitated the expansion of primary health service coverage to 94.5% of the population. In the twelve-month interval from mid-2013 until mid-2014, HMIS reported a total of 2,383,010 malaria illnesses including 1,256,611 outpatient *P. falciparum* malaria illnesses; 16,326 malaria admissions from *P. falciparum*; and fewer than 450 malaria deaths from these public health facilities that respectively represented 5%, 2.4%, and <2.5% of outpatient visits, inpatient admissions, and inpatient deaths from all causes for all age groups. For children aged less than five years, there were 324,203 malaria outpatient visits (includes *P. falciparum* and *P. vivax*), 5,103 inpatient malaria admissions (includes *P. falciparum* or unconfirmed malaria, but does not include *P. vivax* cases), and fewer than 122 (<2.4%) inpatient malaria deaths. For the first time in over fifteen years, malaria deaths were not listed among the top ten causes of inpatient mortality for all age groups, and for children less than five years of age in Ethiopia. Triangulation with previous HMIS reports and with other data from the micro-plan and PHEM indicates that more than 80% of the outpatient and inpatient malaria burden in Ethiopia is among adults and children who are at least five years of age.

The FMOH's PHEM system receives similar reports as the HMIS but includes malaria health post data from district offices on a weekly basis; this PHEM surveillance system now reports about 80% completeness as published in the Annual Review Meeting reports. From July 2013-June 2014, the PHEM reported 2,627,182 total malaria cases among all age groups including 2,210,298 laboratory confirmed cases (1,415,150 *P. falciparum* and 795,148 *P. vivax* cases), and 213 reported malaria deaths among all age groups.

The annual micro-planning survey provided about 99% reporting completeness from 16,786 public health facilities within malarious districts in the interval between July 2013 and June 2014. There were 3,558,360 total malaria cases, including 3,259,119 laboratory-confirmed and 299,241 presumed (i.e., clinically treated) malaria cases. There were 2,286,589 laboratory-confirmed *P. falciparum* outpatient malaria cases, and 972,530 outpatient *P. vivax* cases. In the same reporting period, there were 10,365,782 patients who were examined (i.e., malaria laboratory-tested) for malaria and a calculated total of 10,665,023 suspected malaria cases (note that "suspected" cases were formerly termed "fever cases" per WHO) and 32,530 malaria hospitalizations.

Emerging data from episodic special outbreak investigations and unpublished anecdotes from Ethiopian malaria partners suggest that older boys and men may be at special risk for malaria from occupational and travel-related factors such as engaging in seasonal migrant farm work.

3. Country health system delivery structure and Federal Ministry of Health organization

Ethiopia operates under a federal system of government. Administratively, the country is divided into regional states, zones, districts (*woredas*), and communities/municipalities (*kebeles*) (see Figure 2). There are about 835 districts with different levels of malaria risk in Ethiopia, with an estimated at-risk population of 50.6 million people as per the new stratification (see Table 1 above). The best available proxy for local malaria transmission risk in Ethiopia is household altitude below 2,000 meters (above sea level), since malaria is rarely transmitted at higher elevations (unless there are weather abnormalities and widespread epidemics). Many districts have variable topographical features, with some households within communities located above and below 2,000 meters. Due in part to household locations at various altitudes and distances from efficient malaria vector breeding sites, malaria risk is unevenly distributed within many districts and *kebeles*.

Figure 2: Administrative zones and districts, Ethiopia

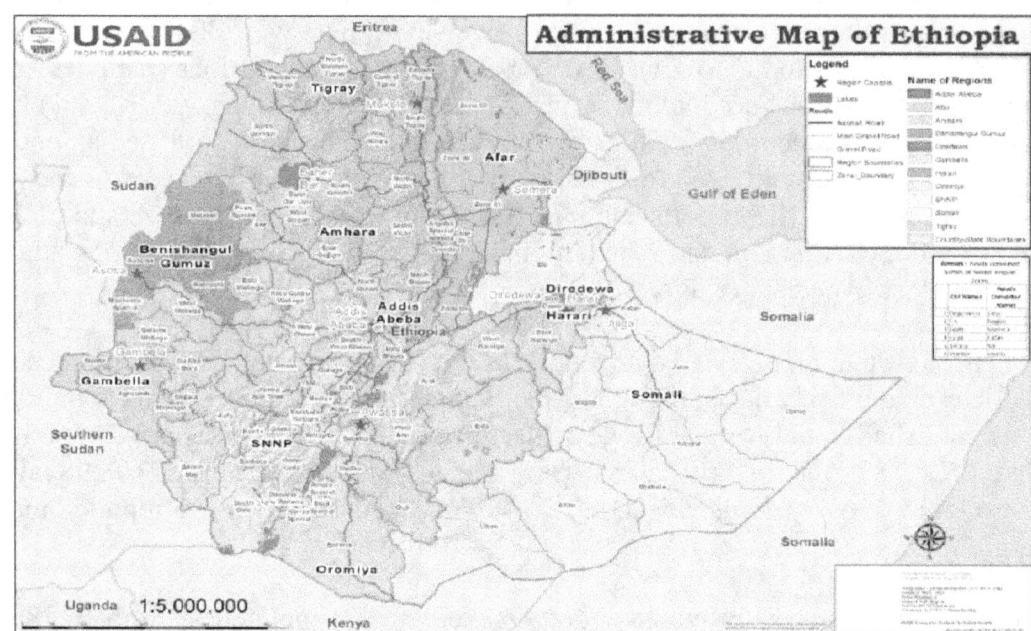

The health care service delivery system in Ethiopia has been re-organized into a three-tier system. The lowest tier is known as the Primary Health Care Unit, which is composed of one district hospital (covering 60,000-100,000 people), health centers (1 per 25,000 people), and their satellite health posts (1 per 5,000 people). The second tier is the General Hospital, covering a catchment population of 1-1.5 million people, and the third, tertiary health care level, is the Specialized Hospital, covering a population of 3.55 million people. All the regional states, including Oromia Regional Health Bureau (ORHB), share the same health system organizational structure. The health center provides comprehensive primary health care services and backup to the health posts by accepting referral cases, while district and general hospitals provide secondary health care. Health centers typically can provide inpatient services for up to two malaria patients, and they are equipped with injectable artesunate for severe malaria treatment.

According to the 2013/2014 Health Sector Development Plan (HSDP) IV Annual Performance Report from the Annual Review Meeting, currently there are a total of 150 public hospitals, 3,335 health centers, and 16,251 health posts, and about 38,000 trained health extension workers (HEWs) in Ethiopia.

Oromia, Ethiopia's largest Regional State (Figure 3), had a population of 32 million people in 2014 with 304 districts organized into 18 rural zones and six urban/zone level 'special towns' and 7,021 *kebeles*. According to a 2014 report, there were 43 hospitals, 1,098 functional health centers, and 6,052 health posts operated by the Government of Ethiopia (GoE) in Oromia Region. There are also 8 hospitals, 5 health centers and 115 health stations under other governmental organizations (e.g., teaching or armed services hospitals). In addition, there are 3 private hospitals and 1,639 private clinics, of which 1,343 are lower level, 253 are medium level, and 43 are higher level.

Figure 3: Zones, districts (*woredas*), and administrative areas within Oromia Regional State, Ethiopia, 2014

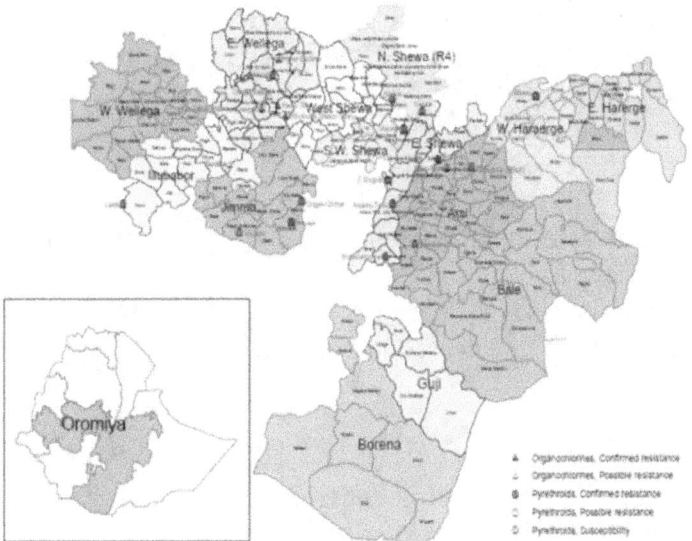

The typical health post is staffed by two HEWs delivering 16 selected health packages, including one health package on malaria [http://cnhde.ei.columbia.edu/training/index.html]. Health extension workers are paid FMOH staff; they undergo a one-year training program after having received a high school diploma, and usually originate from the communities they serve. The HEWs focus on preventive services; however, they also provide curative health care services for malaria, pneumonia, and diarrhea using the integrated community case management (iCCM) approach of evidence-based diagnostic and treatment algorithms. For malaria, HEWs have been trained to confirm and report malaria diagnoses among clinically evaluated acutely ill patients using malaria multispecies RDTs. Severe malaria cases are to be referred to the next appropriate health facility, with initial stabilization with rectal artesunate. The HEWs are encouraged to consider other diagnostic possibilities for patients who test negative by malaria RDT, and to avoid empiric treatment with antimalarials when malaria RDTs are available. The HEWs are also expected to supervise seasonal health activities, including social and behavior change communication (SBCC) and mass vaccination campaigns, participate in surveys and a range of other community health activities. The HEWs work closely with the health development army (HDA), a network of women that oversee up to five households to deliver malaria messages, to perform these tasks. Additionally, HEWs have become more directly involved in supervising IRS spray teams and door-to-door mobilization for IRS. The FMOH envisages decentralizing IRS operations to the primary health care unit, where HEWs would be responsible for supervising the operations in their catchment area (*kebele*). The FMOH is scaling up this community-based IRS (CB IRS) practice in a stepwise approach. Currently, HEWs are primarily responsible for organizing and executing IRS operations in 6 of 36 PMI-supported IRS districts.

4. National malaria control strategy

The updated malaria NMSP for the years 2014–2020 was finalized in August 2014, which was envisioned to be aligned with the next 20 years health sector transformation plan (HSTP) and submitted along with the Concept Note for the Global Fund NFM application. A draft HSTP is near approval and is expected to replace the HSDP IV. The updated malaria strategic plan was developed following the MIS 2011 and the national malaria program review as well as in response to discussions and recommendations following a consultative meeting with key in-country and international malaria stakeholders as a part of the Global Fund's NFM. The following goals and objectives are set out in the new NMSP.

Goals:
- By 2020, to achieve near zero malaria deaths (no more than one confirmed malaria death per 100,000 population at risk) in Ethiopia.
- By 2020, to reduce malaria cases by 75% from baseline of 2013.
- By 2020, to eliminate malaria in selected low transmission areas.

Strategic Objectives:

1. By 2020, all households living in malaria endemic areas will have the knowledge, attitudes and practice towards malaria prevention and control.
2. By 2017 and beyond, 100% of suspected malaria cases are diagnosed using RDTs or microscopy within 24 hours of fever onset.
3. By 2015 and beyond, 100% of confirmed malaria cases are treated according to the national guidelines.
4. By 2015 and beyond, ensure and maintain universal access of the population at risk to at least one type of globally recommended anti-vector intervention.
5. By 2020, achieve and sustain zero indigenous transmission of malaria in 50 selected districts.
6. By 2020, 100% complete data and evidence will be generated at all levels within designated time periods to facilitate appropriate decision-making.

The new NMSP (2014-2020) takes into account the findings of the 2007 and 2011 MIS, which measured the coverage and utilization of key malaria interventions by at-risk populations. Community empowerment and social mobilization are therefore given high priority among the malaria control strategies in the new Plan. Similarly, malaria diagnosis, case management, disease surveillance and epidemic control are geared to serve Ethiopia's goal of shrinking malaria endemicity and achieving zero indigenous transmission in 50 districts by 2020. To translate this plan into action, in May 2015, the FMOH, in collaboration with partners and stakeholders, held a two-day workshop to learn from in-country and other country experiences and to help build consensus on the way forward. Accordingly, Ethiopia has already adapted the approach that all malaria diagnosis is to be based on diagnostic testing, either by microscopy or RDTs, and treatment of malaria cases is to be guided by the result of the confirmatory diagnosis. Surveillance will expand to include individual cases to identify the sources of infection and to limit further local transmission.

The Ethiopian national guidelines for malaria diagnosis and treatment, vector control, and malaria epidemic detection and response that were last updated in 2012 are available on the FMOH website. Additional treatment guideline updates are expected by late 2015 to reflect the recently published WHO Guidelines for the Treatment of Malaria.

5. Updates in the strategy section

Although much of Ethiopia remains at risk of malaria, routine surveillance data from the last decade have noted declining malaria outpatient morbidity and inpatient mortality trends. Based on this progress, the NMSP has set a new strategic goal of eliminating malaria in select low transmission areas by 2020. The FMOH 2015 draft Sub-national Malaria Elimination Guideline describes some aspects of the pathway from "scale-up for impact" to sustained malaria control to pre-elimination to malaria elimination. As a result, in May 2015, detailed discussions were held amongst FMOH NMCP, Ethiopian Public Health Institute (EPHI), PMI, Global Fund, and other malaria partners to clarify the activities that will support the NMSP's goal of eliminating malaria in selected low transmission areas by 2020.

6. Integration, collaboration, and coordination

Maternal, neonatal and child health, family planning, and reproductive health:

Following the first National Family Fertility Survey conducted in 1990, the USG started supporting the FMOH in the delivery of key Maternal, Neonatal and Child Health (MNCH), family planning, and nutrition services at the community level including expanded immunization, family planning, essential nutrition actions, malaria prevention, control and case management, promotion of antenatal care (ANC), and water, sanitation and hygiene. These interventions are delivered through health centers, health posts, and households and focus on rural, peri-urban, and hard-to-reach populations. To date, the program has trained over 60,000 community health volunteers, provided assistance to over 15,000 HEWs, and has reached over 32 million people (35% of the Ethiopian population) in 301 districts in 8 of the country's 9 regional states and parts of Somali Region. Under the Feed the Future Initiative, the USG will also continue to integrate health, agriculture, and humanitarian assistance and livelihood sector platforms to maximize impact on nutrition.

Most of PMI's support to these activities is being implemented through partners supporting the rural HEWs and the recently scaled up HDA at community levels with a multi-agency collaborative approach using Global Health Initiative (GHI) and United States Agency for International Development (USAID) processes and structures. PMI uses this platform to reach the most at-risk communities in malaria diagnosis and treatment, epidemic detection and response, and also to promote best practices in malaria case management by HEWs at health posts, including use of iCCM clinical algorithms.

PEPFAR, GHI, and other USG programs:

PMI is working with PEPFAR within the GHI framework through USAID and Centers for Disease Control and Prevention (CDC) structures, to harmonize the Ethiopia FY 2015 Country Operational Plan, with the USAID Health team's Operational Plan for Family Health and Infectious Diseases to ensure the respective plans complement and strengthen each other. Thus, currently approximately 20% of PMI's budget is allocated to 'wrap around' activities with PEPFAR, i.e., either through the co-funding of an award or by leveraging resources that have been established through previous PEPFAR support (e.g., laboratory infrastructure strengthening overlapping with HIV and tuberculosis diagnosis, malaria SBCC harmonization with other health messages, pharmaceutical system and supply chain strengthening, and pharmaceutical quality management). PMI also has had important cooperative malaria LLIN hang-up projects with U.S. Department of Defense Combined Joint Task Force-Horn of Africa, and has other malaria prevention projects with Peace Corps and CDC (i.e., Field Epidemiology Laboratory Training Program (FELTP), known as EFETP in Ethiopia) within the GHI context.

Coordination with other partners:

The Malaria Control Support Team (MCST) provides coordinated malaria technical support to the national and regional programs and is comprised of members of the FMOH, donors and international organizations, including PMI, governmental and non-governmental organizations (NGOs), and academia. The primary task of the MCST is to support the FMOH and regional health bureaus (RHBs) through ongoing technical assistance, resource mobilization, support to epidemic preparedness and response, and malaria pre-elimination. The MCST provides a common forum to share roles and responsibilities, avoid duplication and discuss technical and programmatic issues and priorities.

Part of the MCST is the Technical Advisory Committee (TAC), which includes the main malaria stakeholders in the country, i.e., FMOH, EPHI, Ethiopian universities, Malaria Control and Evaluation Partnership in Africa, Malaria Consortium, PMI, UNICEF, WHO, etc. PMI is also a member and currently the co-chair of the TAC, representing a technical core of the MCST which advises the FMOH on policy and program implementation issues, providing technical assistance on an ad hoc basis, and assisting with malaria program integration issues. PMI has also been instrumental in the development and finalization of the NMSP 2014-2020, five Global Fund proposals (Rounds 7, 8 and 10, Round 2 Rolling Continuation Channel, and Transitional Funding Mechanism (TFM)) as well as the recent NFM concept note, and the development and updating of in-country guidelines and strategies. Non-PMI funded malaria partners and other health donors as well as experts from the Global Fund were consulted to inform this FY 2016 MOP document.

In addition, PMI is supporting coordination of malaria research stakeholders, academia and FMOH to fill the gap between the implementation of emerging malaria knowledge and research and the adoption of best malaria practices by researchers, practitioners, policymakers, and organizations involved in the prevention and control of the disease. Resolving this gap would serve to increase the benefits of quality research to improve prevention and control, and avoid duplication of efforts and waste of resources.

7. PMI goal, objectives, strategic areas, and key indicators

Under the new PMI Strategy for 2015-2020, the U.S. Government's goal is to work with PMI-supported countries and partners to further reduce malaria deaths and substantially decrease malaria morbidity, towards the long-term goal of elimination. Building upon the progress to date in PMI-supported countries, PMI will work with NMCPs and partners to accomplish the following objectives by 2020:

1. Reduce malaria mortality by one-third from 2015 levels in PMI-supported countries, achieving a greater than 80% reduction from PMI's original 2000 baseline levels.
2. Reduce malaria morbidity in PMI-supported countries by 40% from 2015 levels.

3. Assist at least five PMI-supported countries to meet the World Health Organization's (WHO) criteria for national or sub-national pre-elimination.[1]

These objectives will be accomplished by emphasizing five core areas of strategic focus:
1. Achieving and sustaining scale of proven interventions
2. Adapting to changing epidemiology and incorporating new tools
3. Improving countries' capacity to collect and use information
4. Mitigating risk against the current malaria control gains
5. Building capacity and health systems towards full country ownership

To track progress toward achieving and sustaining scale of proven interventions (area of strategic focus #1), PMI will continue to track the key indicators recommended by the Roll Back Malaria Monitoring and Evaluation Reference Group (RBM MERG) as listed below:

- Proportion of households with at least one ITN
- Proportion of households with at least one ITN for every two people
- Proportion of children under five years old who slept under an ITN the previous night
- Proportion of pregnant women who slept under an ITN the previous night
- Proportion of households in targeted districts protected by IRS
- Proportion of children under five years old with fever in the last two weeks for whom advice or treatment was sought
- Proportion of children under five with fever in the last two weeks who had a finger or heel stick
- Proportion receiving an ACT among children under five years old with fever in the last two weeks who received any antimalarial drugs
- Proportion of women who received two or more doses of IPTp for malaria during ANC visits during their last pregnancy

---

[1] http://whqlibdoc.who.int/publications/2007/9789241596084_eng.pdf

8. Progress on coverage/impact indicators to date

Table 2: Evolution of Key Malaria Indicators in Ethiopia from 2005 to 2011

Indicator	2005, DHS, National	2007, MIS, National <2000m	2007, MIS, National <2500m	2007, MIS, Oromia, <2500m	2011, MIS, National <2000m	2011, MIS, Oromia, <2000m
% Households with at least one ITN	3.4	65.3	53.1	41	54.8	43.7
% Households with at least one ITN for every two people	-	36.6	29.5	21.4	23.6	17.3
% Children under five (U5) who slept under a mosquito net or LLIN the previous night	1.6	41.2	13.3	23.6	38.0	26.5
% of children U5 who slept under mosquito net or LLIN that **own** a net or LLIN the previous night		60.0	50.6	56.5	64.7	55.4
% Pregnant women who slept under a mosquito net or LLIN the previous night	1.1	42.5	17.7	28.7	34.7	26.7
% pregnant women who slept under any mosquito net or LLIN that **own** net or LLIN the previous night		66.2	64.3	73.9	63.8	64
% women age 15-49 years who heard of malaria	-	79.5	74.6	68.6	71.3	68.7
% women age 15-49 years who recognize fever as malaria symptom	-	50.8	44.4	31.6	76.0	71.3
% women age 15-49 years who report mosquito bite as malaria cause	-	41.1	35.8	32.0	71.2	73.2
% women age 15-49 years who report that ITNs provide malaria protection	-	38.2	32.8	22.6	63.4	65.5
% Households protected by at least one LLIN or IRS	-	-	-	-	71.7	63.7
% Households in targeted districts protected by IRS in past 12 months	2.3	20.0	14.2	12.5	46.6	43.0
% Children under five years of age with fever in the last two weeks	-	24.0	22.3	21.5	19.7	15.4
% Children under five years of age with fever in the last two weeks who received any antimalarial drugs	0.7	11.9	9.5	6.6	32.6	38.8
% Children under age 5 years of age who took an antimalarial drug the same or next day	-	4.8	3.9	1.3	8.5	13.8

Indicator	2005, DHS, National	2007, MIS, National <2000m	2007, MIS, National <2500m	2007, MIS, Oromia, <2500m	2011, MIS, National <2000m	2011,MIS, Oromia, <2000m
% Children < age five years who took an antimalarial drug on same or next day	-	16.3	15.4	16.4	51.3	59.5
% Women who received two or more doses of IPTp during their last pregnancy in the last two years (Note: IPTp is not routinely performed, per NMCP policy)	N/A	N/A	N/A	N/A	N/A	N/A
Prevalence by microscopy of *P. falciparum* (%) in children under five years of age	-	0.7	0.5	0.1	1.0	0.2
Prevalence by microscopy of *P. vivax* (%) in children under five years of age	-	0.3	0.2	0.2	0.3	0.3

PMI supported a malaria impact evaluation that assessed progress in malaria control since 2000. Additional details from this report were published in the FY 2015 MOP. Official Ethiopian estimates published in World Malaria Report 2008 were 12.4 million annual malaria cases in 2006, 41,000 annual deaths among all ages, and 25,000 annual deaths among children under five years of age. The Ethiopian NMSP 2014-2020 estimated that there were only 5 million malaria cases in 2013. As of 2013, the PMI-supported malaria impact evaluation estimated that major progress had been made, resulting in about 3,000-6,000 annual malaria deaths (5/100,000) among all age groups in Ethiopia, with 1,000 to 2,000 of these occurring among children under five years of age, with malaria representing less than 1% of all deaths among children under five years of age. The updated NMSP (2014-2020) aims to reduce malaria deaths to about 600-1,000 annually among all age groups (1/100,000) by 2020. This ambitious goal for malaria mortality reduction can only be attained through continued government and donor support and the concerted action among many malaria partners in Ethiopia.

9. Other relevant evidence on progress

Although malaria remains among the leading causes of Ethiopian outpatient morbidity and inpatient morbidity, it is declining as a relative cause of inpatient mortality, especially among children under five years of age, according to HMIS data. Since the most recent published surveillance data were from mid-2014, in the interim, the malaria situation in Ethiopia appears to be stable and steadily improving based upon the absence of reports of epidemics or focal case build-ups. Access to prompt rational malaria case management—including near-universal laboratory-based diagnosis in remote rural areas—has improved dramatically over the last decade. Concurrently, surveillance systems appear to be more accurately and nearly completely documenting public sector health facility malaria morbidity and mortality. These credible surveillance data and recently strengthened health information systems will be essential to guide malaria control efforts more rapidly and accurately, and the interpretation of malaria trends should be easier in future years than it was during the previous decade. Ongoing discussions are needed with

FMOH to coordinate pre-elimination activities together with other donor-supported projects that continue to help shrink the malaria transmission map in Ethiopia.

10. Challenges and opportunities

Ethiopia is a low-income country, with an estimated population of 91.2 million in 2014, with 15.5 million children under the age of five years, 205,000 annual deaths among children under five years, 68/1,000 live births under five mortality rate, 3.5 million annual births, and a maternal mortality ratio of 420/100,000 live births. The Ethiopian health systems have many weaknesses in infrastructure and human resources. The potential for malaria epidemics and the highly variable rain patterns with complex geographical features complicate forecasts for malaria commodities at the remote rural community level, and provide challenges to maintaining medical supply chains. Ethiopia's vulnerability to climate change, *El Niño* rain and temperature patterns, and focal and regional drought and flooding conditions create an expectation that certain communities will be displaced and affected by food scarcity every year. Because of Ethiopia's enormous agriculture-led development and mining industries in malaria risk areas in recent years, there have been massive seasonal population influxes with predominantly male migratory labor forces moving to the western lowlands. The health services in these areas are not yet developed and even district health programs are not capable of providing the required services for these seasonal workers. This creates a significant threat where malaria can spread to other parts of the country, including traditionally non-malarious areas. Emergence and spread of insecticide resistance pose constant threats to the Ethiopian malaria situation.

Opportunities include rapid improvement of many health metrics over the last decade, and the establishment of new rural health centers and rural health posts staffed with paid HEWs that have tripled malaria case reporting and prompt case management with laboratory based diagnosis and effective medicines including ACTs. Ethiopia has enjoyed robust economic growth and improved productivity over the last decade, and has had consistently reliable donor support from the Global Fund, PMI, and Millennium Development Grant Fund, as well as high quality technical support from various malaria partners, including WHO and UNICEF. Low malaria transmission in the highland fringe areas provides discrete areas for enhanced pre-elimination activities that should further shrink the malaria transmission map in Ethiopia in accordance with the FMOH's NMSP (2014-2020).

III. OPERATIONAL PLAN

PMI supports all elements of the NMCP's national malaria strategy in Ethiopia, and specifically aligns with GoE's HSDP IV (2011–2015), draft HSTP 2015, and NMSP (2014–2020). PMI's support strategy for Ethiopia has evolved since PMI began its activities in FY 2008, but remains consistent with the USG's updated PMI, GHI, and USAID global health strategies, and with country strategies within the US Embassy/Addis Ababa and USAID/Ethiopia. PMI funding is targeted to fill gaps in activities that are not already supported by the FMOH, Global Fund, or other donors. PMI support has been flexible and responsive to the FMOH's evolving needs, including the occasional reprogramming of resources to provide critical malaria commodities that were not adequately funded by other sources. Additionally, PMI has provided considerable technical support and expertise for FMOH through malaria technical experts within CDC/Atlanta, USAID/Washington, and the various implementing partners and collaborative support with the Global Fund, academia, and international development organizations.

Beginning in FY 2008, funding limitations required PMI to initially focus support primarily within the Oromia Regional State, based upon earlier evidence that Oromia Regional State had the highest relative malaria burden and gaps in malaria services compared to other Regional States. Initially, there was substantial funding from the Global Fund and availability of other malaria partners to support most malaria-related activities in the other Regional States. However, it was later evident that several other Regional States, including Southern Nations, Nationalities, and Peoples' Region (SNNPR), had consistently higher malaria burdens compared to Oromia Regional State. The availability of increased PMI funding for malaria activities since 2010 and progress made in Oromia Region allowed PMI to progressively support additional NMCP activities outside of Oromia Regional State, including procurement of malaria commodities to fill periodic gaps in Global Fund support and FMOH resources.

1. Insecticide-treated nets

NMCP/PMI objectives

In line with the Ethiopia HSDP IV and the draft HSTP, it is FMOH policy that all citizens have the right to appropriate health care and protection from malaria. The FMOH's NMSP 2014-2020 ensures universal coverage of ITNs (i.e., one ITN per 1.8 persons or for logistic purposes for 2 persons), and improved utilization and care of ITNs through social behavior change communication (SBCC) activities. For subsequent discussions in this MOP, ITNs in Ethiopia are universally assumed to be long-lasting insecticidal nets (LLINs). To achieve this universal coverage, the NMSP calculated a need for 29.6 million LLINs nationally to protect all households who are living within areas with ongoing malaria transmission in 2015; since 40% of Ethiopians live within malaria-free areas, this leaves 60% of Ethiopians who are targeted for universal coverage. The LLINs, once distributed and hung within households, are expected to be effective at preventing malaria transmission for three years. As seen in Table 1, above, nearly all of the 50.5 million people at significant malaria risk live within households at altitudes of <2000m. As Ethiopia moves to pre-elimination by 2020 in targeted areas, maximizing use of LLINs is deemed to be essential for sustained malaria prevention.

Ethiopia is planning to distribute nearly 29.6 million LLINs with Global Fund and PMI support to achieve universal coverage by 2015 through mass campaigns (Table 3). As coverage gaps start to appear after the campaign, subsequent continuous distribution of LLINs, mainly through community-based HEWs, will be used to ensure all malaria-affected families are protected by LLINs from malaria infection. Continuous distribution of LLINs by HEWs will replace worn out/deteriorated or lost nets and cover new households and new household members in all targeted malaria affected communities. This continuous distribution is mainly handled by the health extension program (HEP) in collaboration with the HDA (a network of one model mother representing five households) and local authorities. Health extension workers receive technical assistance and supervision from the district health offices and health centers. Health extension workers identify and confirm the need for LLINs through their routine household visits and from HDA reports. The continuous distribution needs are based on 8% and 20% loss of LLINs in the first and second year of the mass distribution campaign, respectively. These assumptions were used nationally to plan for LLIN needs in 2016 and 2017.

Progress since PMI was launched

Between FY 2007 and FY 2014, PMI procured a total of 16,068,979 LLINs, which were distributed to malaria risk communities. Since 2012, PMI LLIN distribution expanded to other regions beyond Oromia focusing on high risk areas nationally.

Distributions of LLINs for both PMI and Global Fund were based on a nationwide micro-plan developed by PMI in collaboration with the RHBs and FMOH and other malaria partners in the country since 2011. The micro-planning exercise that PMI supported collects district- and *kebele*-level data on the number of malaria cases and key malaria commodities including LLINs. For LLINs, each annual micro-planning meeting compiles records of the number of LLINs previously distributed within the last three years, and documents LLINs that were more than three years old and thus need to be replaced. The micro-plan estimates the 12-month need and gap of LLINs based on district-level sub-populations with malaria risk (generally by *kebele*), malaria morbidity, and LLIN data. In addition to replacement of LLINs, the number of "gap filling" nets was calculated by quantifying the number of new households (resulting from population growth rates) and malaria affected households that never received nets in previous distributions.

Progress during the last 12-18 months

The FMOH's Global Fund NFM proposal identified the need for 29,584,492 LLINs in 2015 to achieve universal coverage. The resources available from TFM (13.9 million LLINs) and PMI (FY 2013 and FY 2014 funding 6.8 million LLINs) will provide 20,802,724 of this total requirement. The FMOH through Global Fund Round 8 Phase 2 and TFM funding also procured another 8.8 million LLINs. It is now anticipated all Global Funds LLINs will be delivered to the country before the end of 2015.

In early 2015, PMI procured and delivered 4.3 million LLINs (a portion of the 6.8 million LLINs mentioned above) using FY 2013 and FY 2014 funds and these were distributed to high risk malaria districts in Oromia, Amhara, and Tigray Regions. The PMI FY 2015 MOP planned to purchase an additional 4.785 million LLINs when these funds become available in order to replace worn out nets after universal coverage is attained in late 2015. In 2016 and 2017, PMI will be the only source for LLIN procurement. As per the LLIN gap analysis, the surplus of 1,649,044 LLINs in FY 2016 is to be carried over to 2017, thus decreasing the anticipated gap in 2017 to 1,307,927 LLINs.

24

In addition to replacement of LLINs, the number of "gap filling" nets was calculated by quantifying the number of new households and malaria affected households that never received LLINs in previous distributions. The micro-plan is used by FMOH for distribution of LLINs for both PMI and Global Fund procured LLINs in the country.

Table 3: LLIN Gap Analysis

Calendar Year	2015	2016	2017
Total Targeted Population	53,252,086	54,636,640	56,057,192
Continuous Distribution Needs			
Channel #1: ANC			
Channel #2: EPI			
Channel #3: Community distribution through HEWs		3,135,956	6,956,971
Estimated Total Need for Continuous		3,135,956	6,956,971
Mass Distribution Needs			
2015 mass distribution campaign	29,584,492		
Estimated Total Need for Campaigns	29,584,492		
Total Calculated Need: Routine and Campaign	29,584,492	3,135,956	6,956,971
Partner Contributions			
ITNs carried over from previous year			1,649,044
ITNs from FMOH			
ITNs from Global Fund Round (TFM)	13,993,033		
ITNs from Global Fund Round (NFM)	8,781,768		
ITNs planned with PMI funding	6,809,691*	4,785,000**	4,000,000
Total ITNs Available	29,584,492	4,785,000	5,649,044
Total ITN Surplus (Gap)	0	1,649,044***	(1,307,927)

*2013-14 funding
**PMI LLINs in 2016 are for keep-up campaign using FY 2015 funding.
***Surplus of 1, 649,044 to be carried over to 2017 and procurement is planned to cover the following transmission season.

FMOH believes that the 2015 mass campaign will establish a foundation for the beginning of continuous annual distribution efforts that will require about 11% of LLINs (3,135,956) to be replaced in 2016 and about 24% (6,956,971) in 2017 accounting for net deterioration/loss and population growth for continuous distribution. The NFM states that given no local evidence for the loss rate of nets, the continuous distribution calculated net lost based on RBM Harmonization Working Group recommendation of 8%, 20%, and 50% in the first, second, and third year of distribution, respectively. PMI is currently planning a longitudinal LLIN durability assessment in conjunction with the planned mass campaigns in 2015.

Plans and justification

PMI supports the FMOH policy and distribution plans of LLINs to the most at-risk communities in significant malaria transmission areas as per NMSP 2014-2020 malaria stratification. In addition to the LLIN procurement and distribution, PMI in collaboration with FMOH and other in-country stakeholders are currently assisting with the national micro-planning process for LLIN needs assessment and plans for distribution. The FMOH requested via the Global Fund TFM grant application for 100% LLIN coverage of the at-risk population assuming 1.8 nets per person in 2015, replacing LLINs after three years. In earlier FMOH grant applications, either two LLIN nets per household (averaging five persons) or one net per two persons had been requested.

A LLIN durability study was supported in previous MOPs and will be discussed under the M&E section. The information generated from the LLIN durability assessment will inform the LLIN replacement plans, SBCC activities related to LIIN use, and resource mobilization for LLINs beyond 2017.

Proposed activities with FY 2016 funding: **($13,760,000)**

- **Procurement and distribution of LLINs to districts ($13,160,000):** Due to the pressing need to cover the LLIN gap, PMI will support the procurement and distribution of 4 million LLINs through continuous distribution channels for replacement of worn-out LLINs in priority malaria transmission areas nationally. The LLINs will be delivered to the district level and distributed free to communities mainly through HEWs.

- **LLIN distribution from districts to health posts/communities ($600,000):** PMI will assist districts to transport LLINs from district level to health posts and communities, at approximately $0.15/LLIN. All activities will be coordinated with local authorities and HEWs in order to ensure that engagement of targeted districts is maximized, LLINs are distributed before malaria transmission season and communities are educated to use LLINs properly and care for them appropriately.

2. Indoor residual spraying

NMCP/PMI objectives

IRS remains a key area of strategic focus for both PMI and the FMOH. In its NMSP (2014-2020), the NMCP's objectives include: "to ensure and maintain universal access of the population at risk to at least one type of globally recommended anti-vector intervention by 2020," and "to increase and maintain IRS coverage to 100% in IRS-targeted districts by 2020." According to the FMOH's new NMSP malaria stratification based upon API, only 17% of the districts in the country will be targeted yearly for IRS, specifically 32% of the highland fringe areas where the risk of malaria is low (13% of total) but risk of epidemics is higher, and the areas at lower altitudes with the highest malaria burden (13% of total). Due to the varied topography and heterogeneity of malaria transmission within districts, not all communities in a specific district will be targeted for spraying. Specific IRS-targeted communities are selected based on malaria case load, altitude (< 2000 meters), presence of nearby *Anopheles* breeding sites, agriculture and water development practices, epidemic records, and other economic or social factors. The selection of communities for IRS will be refined every year within the IRS targeted districts. In general, PMI does not conduct blanket spraying in supported districts in Ethiopia but follows the FMOH guidance for sub-district targeting for spraying based on the criteria outlined above. The selection of areas is done at the district level with reference to incidence data collected and collated at the district level. The Government takes the lead in deciding which areas will receive IRS each year. Successful implementation of IRS following the new stratification requires strong advocacy and training of managers and health personnel at different levels.

Malaria transmission in Ethiopia is seasonal, lasting for about three months after the main rainy season, from September to November. Depending on the residual life of the insecticide used and timing of spray operations, one spray round per year could give the required protection against malaria. As IRS has been a long-standing malaria control practice in the country, the FMOH is implementing IRS in all regions across the country. In 2013/2014, the FMOH has conducted spraying in more than 4.8 million structures inhabited by more than 12 million people.

Progress since PMI was launched

The PMI-supported IRS program in Ethiopia has expanded significantly from its initial coverage of 316,000 structures in 2008, peaking at 858,657 structures sprayed in 2011 (Figure 4, Table 4). Since 2008, PMI has been providing targeted IRS to high malaria burden *kebeles* in PMI-supported districts according to the national guidelines. PMI's IRS coverage increased from 19 districts in 2008 to 50 districts in 2011. In 2011, PMI and ORHB began implementation of a district graduation process, whereby districts that had already received PMI support for two or more years and were considered to have sufficient capacity to assume greater financial and technical responsibility for the spray program were graduated from full PMI support. By 2012, 24 districts were considered fully graduated and only received minimal support for micro-planning, supportive supervision, and the provision of IRS equipment to fill gaps. For the districts to be considered for graduation the burden of malaria should be lower than others; the districts should have sufficient financial resources and technical expertise to run IRS on their own; and possess adequate environmental compliance facilities, storage, equipment and supplies. Hence, the bulk of IRS-related financial and programmatic support was taken over by the graduated districts. PMI continued to provide full IRS support in the remaining 36 districts. The rationale for this graduation approach is that as districts build capacity through extended PMI support over two to three years, it is believed that they will be able to sustain IRS operations with their own resources, and PMI funds could support IRS at the national level or in other districts.

PMI has been supporting insecticide resistance and entomological monitoring activities since 2008 and the FMOH used the findings to discontinue the use of dichloro-diphenyl-trichloroethane (DDT) and pyrethroid insecticides for IRS in the country due to widespread resistance.

Figure 4: IRS results in PMI-supported districts of Oromia Region, Ethiopia, 2008–2014

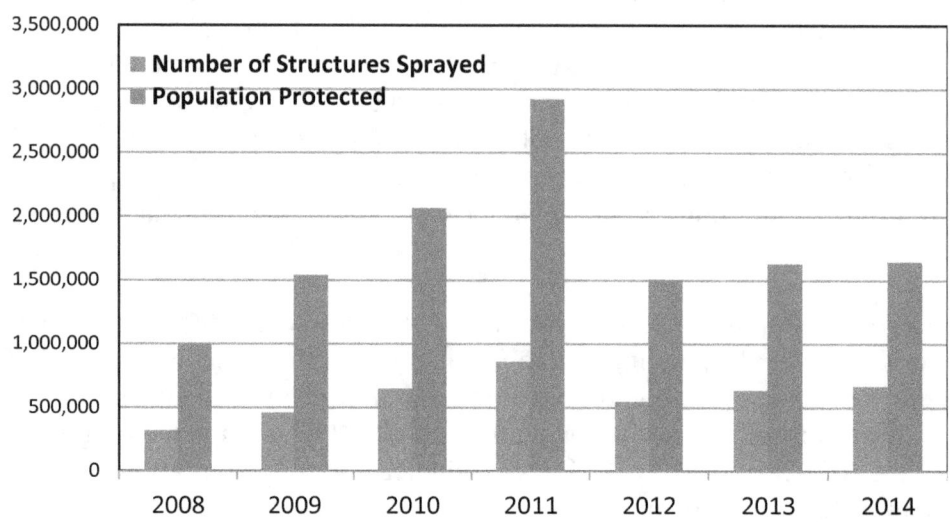

Table 4: PMI-supported IRS activities (2008-2017)

Year	Number of Districts Sprayed	Insecticide Used	Number of Structures Sprayed	Coverage Rate (%)	Population Protected
2008	19	DDT	316,829	92.0	1,000,526
2009	23	DDT	459,402	91.8	1,539,163
2010	30	Deltamethrin	646,870	96.5	2,064,389
2011	50	Deltamethrin + Bendiocarb	858,657	98.6	2,920,469
2012	36	Deltamethrin + Bendiocarb	547,421	98.8	1,506,273
2013	36	Bendiocarb	635,528	99.6	1,629,958
2014	36	Bendiocarb	667,236	99.5	1,647,099
2015*	36	Bendiocarb (28 dist.) + Pirimiphos-methyl CS (8 dist.)	670,303		1,654,670
2016**	26	TBD	484,107		1,195,040
2017**	26	TBD	484,107		1,195,040

* Represents targets based on the draft 2015 IRS work plan.

** Represents projected targets based on national strategic plan and/or discussions with the NMCP.

Progress during the last 12-18 months

IRS Operations: In 2014, PMI supported the spraying of 667,236 structures and protected 1,647,099 people from malaria in 36 districts of Oromia Region, achieving a 99.5% coverage rate. Nearly 2,900 people were trained to deliver IRS during this campaign. The insecticide used in PMI-supported districts in 2014 was bendiocarb while the FMOH used both bendiocarb and propoxur. On the basis of a PMI-supported study of bendiocarb decay rates, the FMOH has agreed for PMI to pilot pirimiphos-methyl CS spraying in 8 out of 36 PMI supported districts in 2015. Lessons learned regarding local suitability, effectiveness, ease of use, and cost of spraying pirimiphos-methyl CS will be drawn from this pilot to advise its future use at larger scale.

District Graduation: In 2014, PMI continued providing two levels of support to districts following a system that began in 2012. Of the 60 districts supported, 24 districts were considered "graduated" and received minimal support, while 36 districts received full support from PMI. Full support includes: procurement of insecticide; operational funds; transportation; rehabilitation of district storage facilities; soak pits; personal protective equipment; environmental compliance; information, education, and communication (IEC) and social mobilization; training on IRS techniques; and use and maintenance of spray pumps. Graduated districts receive only minimal PMI support, which includes: micro-planning consultations; a limited supply of equipment; and technical assistance including environmental compliance monitoring, IRS operations, and supportive supervision.

Community-Based IRS (CB IRS): The involvement of HEWs in IRS as part of the community-based IRS strategy, as indicated in the 2011–2014 NMSP and the new NMSP (2014-2020), further underscores expanding the use of the HEP in the implementation of IRS. This was also elaborated in the national malaria prevention and control guidelines (FMOH third edition, 2012). In 2012, the FMOH requested that PMI pilot the feasibility of integrating IRS into the existing HEP and decentralizing the organization of spray operations from the district to the community level in one district. PMI expanded CB IRS to six districts in 2013 with the aim to assess the scalability of the approach, including the level of supervision required to ensure compliance with standards for environmental health and safety, the ability to maintain a high quality of spraying, and ensuring adequate stock management and sustainability. These same six districts were supported to continue CB IRS operations in 2014. In the 2013 and 2014 spray rounds, the population protected through CB IRS was 373,176 (99.4%) and 386,935 (96.5%), respectively. The performance of the CB IRS approach was evaluated in 2013 and 2014 to assess if it met the required quality and compliance standards. The evaluation findings were positive; it concluded that CB IRS could be an alternative approach to the district-based IRS operations and could be more sustainable in the long run.

Obsolete DDT Removal: Accumulation of obsolete DDT across the country, including in PMI-supported districts, has been a major challenge since the use of DDT for IRS was discontinued in 2010. PMI has made a significant effort to assist the FMOH by committing to the removal of 80 tons of DDT from 60 PMI-supported districts in collaboration with FMOH and ORHB. Remarkable progress was made in 2015; the incineration facility was selected overseas and the removal implementation plan was approved. Training on safe waste removal will be conducted in September 2015 followed by repackaging, collection and shipment, with final incineration of all 80 tons of DDT expected in 2016.

Resistance Monitoring: The FMOH acknowledges that a long-term insecticide resistance management strategy is crucial to ensure continued efficacy of IRS in Ethiopia. The first draft of a National Insecticide Resistance Monitoring and Management Strategy was developed in April and is currently under review. Considering the rapid spread of insecticide resistance among malaria vectors in Ethiopia, the FMOH emphasizes the importance of continuous monitoring of insecticide resistance in the new NMSP (2014-2020).

In 2014, PMI continued supporting vector insecticide resistance monitoring on 11 insecticides from four insecticide classes in eight sites representing different eco-epidemiological settings of the country. Table 5 presents results from seven sites only; the eighth site had insufficient number of mosquitoes to conduct testing. The test results indicated that local vectors are resistant to DDT, pyrethroids, and malathion, which is consistent with previous years' results. It further shows resistance to bendiocarb in two sites and possible resistance in another two sites, which needs closer attention as the level is increasing from year to year. Three sites, namely Alemata, Amibara and Lare, are new sites from the Tigray, Afar, and Gambela Regions, respectively. The test results from these three new sites agree with the previous test results from across the country. The PMI-supported insecticide resistance studies provide trends in the insecticide resistance status over time corresponding to changes in the application of different IRS insecticides following shifts in the insecticide policy of the country. Insecticide resistance monitoring results from the seven sites are presented in Table 5. PMI will be switching to the use of pirimiphos-methyl CS in eight districts in 2015, including in Omonada district where suspected bendiocarb resistance has been documented.

Table 5: Summary of PMI-supported insecticide resistance tests in 2014

Insecticides	Mortality (%) of *An. gambiae* s.l. by site						
	Chewaka (PMI IRS District)	Omonada (PMI IRS District)	Zwai Dugda	Bahirdar	Alemata	Amibara	Lare
DDT	6	7	6	9	25	19	13
Lambda-cyhalothrin	11	39	5	24	58	46	15
Deltamethrin	46	42	11	25	44	45	18
Fenitrothion	100	100	100	100	100	100	100
Malathion	94	73	93	89	89	100	96
Pirimiphos-methyl	100	100	100	100	100	100	100
Propoxur	100	100	100	99	98	100	100
Bendiocarb	100	86	100	87	96	100	92
Permethrin	31	16	3	66	10	19	28
Etofenprox	24	55	29	23	19	87	11
Alpha-cypermethrin	32	35	5	61	77	73	15

Entomological monitoring: In 2014, vector density and behavior studies were conducted before and after spray operations. The results show rapid reduction in the number of malaria vectors resting indoors from pre-spray to the first month after and throughout the fourth month. In Gobu Seyo, the number of mosquitoes resting indoors pre-spray using the pyrethrum spray collection method was 2.8 per household per night, which dropped to 0.75 in the first month post-spray. Likewise, in Seka Chekorsa, the number of *An. gambiae* s.l. collected pre-spray was 7.2 per household per night, which dropped to 0.9 in the first month post-spray. Accordingly, the indoor *An. gambiae* s.l. human biting rate per person per night was reduced from 6.8 to 1 in Gobu Seyo and from 32.3 to 3.8 in Seka Chekorsa during pre-spray and after the fourth month assessment, respectively.

Table 6: Biting rates of *An. gambiae* s.l., August - December 2014

Time	*An. gambiae s.l.* biting rate (per person per night)								
	Gobu Seyo (Intervention)			Seka Chekorsa (Intervention)			Ejaji (Control)		
	In	Out	Total	In	Out	Total	In	Out	Total
August (pre-spray)	6.8	6.8	6.8	32.3	27.3	29.8	1.5	1.5	1.5
September	5.5	8	6.8	9	12.3	10.6	6.3	15.8	11
October	7.3	10	8.6	18.3	26.5	22.4	1.3	0.8	1
November	4.3	7.3	5.8	4.3	9.3	6.8	0.3	0.8	0.5
December	1	1.8	1.4	3.8	6.3	5	1.3	1.8	1.5
Total	5	6	5.9	13.5	16.3	14.9	2.1	4.1	3.1

Carbamate Residual Efficacy: The short residual life of bendiocarb in certain areas has been an issue since 2011 when bendiocarb was first used for IRS in PMI-supported districts. The residual life of bendiocarb on different wall types was studied in 2014 in PMI-supported IRS districts in houses selected for IRS quality check to further document the results and better understand the reasons for the variable residual life. As had been seen from PMI's post-spray data over the past several years, the decay rate of bendiocarb varied significantly on different wall types in 2014. Bendiocarb decayed quickly on mud surfaces compared to other surface types. In Bako Tibe and Gobu Seyo districts, the mortality rates were less than 80% after one month on mud surface with susceptible mosquitoes. During the second month assessment and thereafter in all four sites, mortality rate on mud plastered surfaces dropped to less than 70% with susceptible mosquitoes. Dung, painted and plastic surfaces performed much better than mud surfaces; however, mud is the predominant wall type in the majority of PMI's spray areas (Table 7).

Table 7: Decay rate of bendiocarb on different wall surfaces, 2014

Site	Wall Type	Percent Mortality of *An.gambiae* s.l. (susceptible species)				
		24 Hours	One month	Two Months	Three Months	Four Months
Bako Tibe	Mud	100	75	62	27	34
	Dung	100	100	100	90	68
	Painted	100	100	100	100	100
	Paper Plastered	ND*	100	100	81	48
Gobu Seyo	Mud	100	46	20	48	29
	Dung	100	100	100	100	97
	Painted	100	100	100	100	99
	Paper Plastered	ND	100	100	95	62
Kersa	Mud	100	98	62	19	39
	Painted	100	100	100	90	88
	Plastic	ND	100	100	87	87
Seka Chekorsa	Mud	100	100	63	31	33
	Painted	100	100	100	100	100
	Plastic	ND	100	100	90	87

*ND indicates no data was collected.

<u>Strengthening National Entomological Monitoring Capacity:</u> Building the capacity of district health offices to carry out key entomological monitoring activities as part of their annual malaria intervention plan is considered a crucial step in sustaining these efforts. Staff trained in insecticide resistance testing in 2012 received a follow-up training on the CDC bottle bioassay in November 2013. To further strengthen this capacity, an additional 35 health workers were trained on entomological monitoring from FMOH down to the district level in 2014.

PMI is working closely with Addis Ababa, Jima, and Mekelle Universities to build local capacity in entomological monitoring, and is looking to expand this collaboration to other universities in the future. PMI is conducting insecticide resistance monitoring in collaboration with these universities. PMI supported Jima University in equipping its molecular biology laboratory, vector biology field site, and insectary. Through PMI support, Jima University has developed the capacity to undertake molecular identification of vector species, biochemical assays to determine resistance mechanisms, blood meal analysis, and calculation of entomological inoculation rates.

Plans and justification

With FY 2016 funds, PMI will maintain the FY 2015 level of IRS support and will continue to work closely with the FMOH, ORHB, and other partners. In collaboration with ORHB, PMI will implement the graduation of 10 low malaria burden districts in 2016 using health facility and micro-planning information as per the new NMSP. Prior to graduation, preparatory activities including evaluation of the districts' technical preparedness in IRS operations, consensus building discussions, and securing adequate funding from the district council will take place with adequate lead time in collaboration with ORHB and implementing partners. In addition, through discussions with ORHB, PMI will determine how best to expand PMI's CB IRS implementation beyond the original six districts. With FY 2016 funding, approximately 480,000 structures will be sprayed with full support from PMI in 26 districts, protecting approximately 1.2 million people. In addition, PMI will provide limited support for IRS operations in the 34 graduated districts. PMI will continue to focus on high malaria burden districts in Oromia and support environmental compliance activities, entomological monitoring in sentinel sites and insecticide resistance testing. PMI will collaborate with more local universities particularly in conducting entomological and insecticide resistance monitoring. Malaria elimination has become a key focus of the FMOH, and capacity building of vector control and entomology experts may be a crucial area that PMI may support.

Proposed activities with FY 2016 funding: **($9,464,000)**

- **Indoor residual spray operations, training, and procurement of insecticide for Oromia region ($8,500,000):** With FY 2016 funding, PMI will continue to support ORHB in planning, implementation and evaluation of IRS in 26 districts and minimal support in the 34 graduated districts in Oromia. Based on the evaluation of 2015 operations, the number of structures to be sprayed may be adjusted. PMI will procure required insecticides for spraying in 26 PMI supported districts, support planning, train all spray personnel and undertake all environmental compliance activities highlighted in the supplementary environmental assessment. The exact allocations and specifications of insecticides will be determined upon completion and review of the 2015 IRS activities and the insecticide policy decision of the FMOH.

- **Entomological capacity building and monitoring ($600,000):** Resistance monitoring will be carried out in eight sites using WHO tube tests in different ecological zones of the country to continue documenting what is happening to the resistance status of the vector after change in the insecticide policy. Technical support will be provided to conduct CDC bottle bioassays and to coordinate entomological monitoring activities implemented by the FMOH in sites outside of Oromia. National level vector and insecticide resistance monitoring will be conducted in collaboration with universities in different regions. Behavioral outcomes will be monitored to detect any change in mosquito behavior, particularly outdoor biting changes, in response to the changes in the insecticide used for IRS. Insecticide residual life monitoring to obtain evidence for the selection of the best alternative insecticide also continues to be a priority activity.

- **National level technical assistance for vector control ($250,000):** Provide TA for curriculum development and conduct national level vector control training in the form of a training of trainers program at the federal and regional levels to increase the FMOH's and ORHB's capacity in planning, implementation and management of vector control operations, environmental compliance, safe use of insecticides and poison control. PMI will focus on high disease burden and malaria elimination districts in providing technical assistance and support in-service training.

- **Entomological supplies and equipment ($10,000):** Provide critical supplies, reagents, and equipment for routine entomological monitoring activities and resistance and bionomic studies.

- **Entomological technical assistance ($29,000):** Provide two technical assistance visits from CDC/Atlanta for training, planning, and monitoring entomological activities given the expansion of entomological surveillance up to the national level.

- **Molecular markers of insecticide resistance for *Anopheles arabiensis* ($75,000):** Provide equipment, supplies, and reagents to EPHI and local universities to conduct studies to identify molecular markers that confer insecticide resistance in *Anopheles arabiensis*.

3. Malaria in pregnancy

NMCP/PMI objective

The Ethiopian FMOH's NMSP (2014-2020) does not support intermittent preventive treatment for pregnant women (IPTp) with sulfadoxine-pyrimethamine treatments because of the relatively low intensity of malaria transmission in most of Ethiopia, and the anticipated minimal expected benefits compared with high costs. Malaria in pregnancy in Ethiopia is addressed through: 1) improving prompt access to care and treatment in the iCCM context at rural health posts and at health centers, 2) prioritizing the use of LLINs by pregnant women within households, and 3) enhanced SBCC activities and outreach for pregnant women.

Ethiopia has a relatively low ANC coverage rate compared to other countries in the region. The 2011 DHS indicated that for Ethiopia as a whole, only 34% of mothers received antenatal care from a heath professional for their most recent birth in the five years preceding the survey, although this demonstrated an improvement from the 28% noted in the 2005 DHS. One woman in every five (19%) made four or more ANC visits during the course of her pregnancy, up from 12% in 2005. The median duration of pregnancy at the time of the first antenatal visit is 5.2 months. Furthermore, although pregnant women are at greater risk of severe disease from malaria, overall they have historically represented a small proportion (<3%) of the total number of malaria outpatients and inpatients in Ethiopia, according to annual HMIS surveillance reports. From the last published Integrated Disease Surveillance Report (IDSR) (2008-2009), pregnant women accounted for 1.7% of all reported outpatients with malaria (14,864/1,104,157), 2.9% of reported malaria hospitalizations (574/20,130), and 1.7% of reported inpatient malaria deaths (10/585). Since that time, the IDSR was folded into the PHEM system and specific MIP morbidity and mortality data were no longer published. In a study by Newman et al., a cross-sectional survey of placental parasitemia at a stable (high) malaria transmission site in the sparsely populated Gambela Regional State noted 6.5% prevalence, whereas three other sites in unstable (i.e., low) transmission settings noted only 2.5% prevalence. Because of the relatively low prevalence of malaria infection during pregnancy, IPTp has not been implemented in Ethiopia.

National malaria guidelines were updated in 2012 by the FMOH to include pregnancy-specific treatment guidelines. Consistent with WHO guidance, these guidelines recommend oral quinine for uncomplicated *P. falciparum* malaria in the first trimester, and oral artemether-lumefantrine (AL) for the second and third trimesters. For uncomplicated mono-species *P. vivax* malaria, oral chloroquine is recommended in all trimesters. For severe malaria, IV artesunate for inpatient treatment is recommended. Recent PMI-supported in-vivo monitoring studies have documented that *P. vivax* infected persons in Ethiopia experience an average of two but up to eight relapses within the following 12 months; such illness relapses could be especially harmful to pregnant and breastfeeding women who are unable to take primaquine, have impaired immunity, an impaired nutritional status, and an increased risk of progression to severe or complicated malaria illnesses.

There are few if any LLIN distributions via ANC clinics in Ethiopia, except through a small project that overlaps with PEPFAR. Distribution of LLINs via ANC is not part of the FMOH malaria control strategy. Approaches used by the FMOH to target pregnant women are to: (i) scale-up universal LLIN coverage and encourage pregnant women to use LLINs; and (ii) ensure availability of prompt diagnosis and treatment of clinical malaria cases during pregnancy at health facilities. The LLIN replacement scheme presented in the NMSP is the policy framework for continuous LLIN distribution primarily through the HEP. Nearly all LLINs are distributed by HEWs through mass campaigns every three years and they are instructed to make sure that pregnant mothers and children less than five years of age have preferential access to LLINs in these mass campaigns and educate communities to give priority to pregnant mothers and children, in case LLINs are not sufficient to cover the entire family. Increasing ANC coverage is also one of the FMOH's priorities, and is supported by USAID/Ethiopia MNCH, family planning, and reproductive health funding.

Progress since PMI was launched

In Ethiopia, only 34% of women had received antenatal care from a skilled provider and only 10% were attended by a skilled provider. The most important barrier to access to health services that women of childbearing age mentioned is availability of transport to a facility, followed by lack of money and distance to a health facility, according to the 2011 MIS. Based on the MIS 2007 and 2011, 43% and 35% of pregnant women slept under an LLIN, respectively. A major focus of ANC programs in Ethiopia is providing expanded access to quality healthcare through health centers and health posts, where PMI supported projects since 2008 promoting prompt access to diagnostic and treatment services for pregnant women and in identifying and preferentially distributing LLINs to pregnant women in rural communities.

Progress during the last 12-18 months

PMI provided technical support to update the FMOH's malaria diagnosis and treatment guidelines. These guidelines were reinforced through trainings of HEWs through iCCM rollout that will be completed by late 2015 that also discussed malaria prevention and case management in pregnancy. Minor updates to these guidelines were made in early 2015 partly with PMI technical support. Social behavior change communication messages and training are being developed based on these guidelines. The implementation guidelines based on the updated NMSP are in development.

There are no new surveillance data from IDSR since 2009 concerning trends in the specific burden of malaria in pregnant women or neonates, but as mentioned above, the relatively complete malaria surveillance data that has been available for the general population since 2011 shows the malaria situation has been steadily improving. The Health and Health Related Indicators Report from HMIS data documented "Female" malaria outpatient morbidity from *P. falciparum* in respective years 2011-2012 and 2013-2014 of 599,407 and 470,390; "Female" inpatient morbidity from *P. falciparum* of 11,122 and <9,065; "Female" inpatient mortality of 249 and <185. These HMIS surveillance reports indicate that "Female" morbidity—predominantly of women of childbearing age—has also declined since 2011, along with the general population.

With FY 2015 funds, PMI will continue support for pre-service trainings for midwives, nurse anesthetists, and HEWs to improve malaria case management services for pregnant women. PMI will also conduct operational research (OR) to assess the feasibility of implementing weekly chloroquine suppression for pregnant women with *P. vivax* after completing initial treatment with chloroquine to inform FMOH treatment guideline policy.

Plans and justification

PMI continues to support the current FMOH policies that address pregnant women's special needs through malaria prevention and control, and improving prompt access to malaria diagnosis, and appropriate care and treatment services. Although IPTp itself is not part of the national strategic plan, with FY 2016 funding, PMI will support maternal and perinatal protection from malaria with Focused Antenatal Care Services and Safe Motherhood and Adolescent Reproductive Health through an emphasis on anemia management and the prompt diagnosis and management of acute malaria in pregnant women. To implement these activities, PMI has leveraged the resources of other GHI activities, particularly those supported by USAID/Ethiopia MNCH, family planning, and reproductive health funds, and will ensure that health providers counsel mothers on early detection of anemia and illnesses with fever, the importance of iron and folate supplementation, as well as using a LLIN during pregnancy for the protection of the fetus. This activity will be closely coordinated with PMI support for case management strengthening and supportive supervision for health care workers at health centers and HEWs at health posts.

In the past, the IDSR system collected and reported pregnancy and species-specific malaria surveillance data, but published annual reports since 2009 have not been including these disaggregated data. There has been increased interest in Ethiopia concerning MIP from both the FMOH and Global Fund in recent months. The FMOH's updated NMSP (2014-2020) mentions a plan to assess the burden of MIP in a stable transmission area and to explore the possibility of targeted IPTp activities in high risk regions. PMI encourages these efforts, and will support additional operational research studies (as explained above) that would improve case management practices and provide additional insights into the malaria burden among pregnant women in Ethiopia including the relapse rate for *P. vivax* during pregnancy. PMI will continue to work with the FMOH to identify and review all available MIP surveillance data, and to encourage the future routine collection, analysis, and publication of disaggregated MIP data once again into the FMOH's annual surveillance reports. These enhanced surveillance and operational research efforts would aim to provide an appropriate evidence basis for any possible future health policy changes related to MIP in Ethiopia.

Proposed activities with FY 2016 funding: **($200,000)**

- **Strengthening case management of MIP ($200,000):** Support improving prompt access to malaria diagnosis, and appropriate care and treatment services for pregnant mothers in high disease burden areas in Ethiopia under integrated maternal and child health services.

4. Case management

a. Diagnosis and Treatment

NMCP/PMI objectives

The NMSP 2014–2020 aims for universal access to prompt malaria diagnosis and highly effective treatment services for the entire Ethiopian population, whether living in malaria-free or malaria endemic areas. The NMSP strategic objective for malaria diagnosis specifies that by 2017, 100% of suspected malaria cases are diagnosed using a RDT or microscopy within 24 hours of fever onset. The FMOH's policy is for microscopy to be the primary means of malaria diagnosis at hospitals and health centers, and for malaria RDTs to be the diagnostic method at rural health posts. The NMSP aims to train all HEWs and laboratory professionals in malaria laboratory diagnosis and provide all health posts with RDTs and health centers and hospitals with microscopy and other malaria laboratory commodities and conduct routine external quality assurances.

The NMSP states that ACTs should be available at all public health facilities to treat all *P. falciparum* infections, whereas chloroquine continues to be first-line treatment for *P. vivax* cases. Quinine tablet remains the treatment of choice for uncomplicated *P. falciparum* for pregnant mothers during the first trimester of pregnancy, children under five kilograms body weight, and as second line for treatment failures. Rectal artesunate should be available at rural health posts, and intravenous artesunate or intramuscular injection and intramuscular artemether (alternate) should be available at health centers and hospitals for the treatment of severe malaria. The introduction of dihydroartemisnin-piperaquine as second-line treatment for non-complicated *P. falciparum* and possibly to target mobile populations is being considered. The NMSP promotes primaquine for radical cure of *P. vivax* and also single dose treatment for gametocytocidal activity against *P. falciparum*, where appropriate.

The NMSP aims to train 100% of the HEWs in the necessary skills to properly assess, classify, and manage as per iCCM guideline and protocols. The MIS 2011 survey suggests that about 29% of people initially receive care for febrile illnesses through the private sector. However, the capacity of the private sector to manage malaria well is limited, and they lack trained and competent health workforce, updated tools, and malaria commodities i.e., ACTs, RDTs, microscopy tools, as well as rectal and IV artesunate.

Through USG support, largely PEPFAR, the Government of Ethiopia has recognized the importance of the private sector as a source of health care for many people. This is evidenced by the recent establishment of public-private partnerships in health units in the FMOH; inclusion of representatives from the private health sector in development of new licensing and quality standards by the country's health regulatory agency; inclusion of the private health sector as one of the six "pillars" in the country's new vision for primary health care; and recognition of the new private health facility associations. In addition to the monetary benefit that they get through consultations and diagnosis fees, the private health sector is also obtaining free commodities and supplies for diseases of public health importance through the host government's supply chain management system. Private sector will not charge patients for free commodities received from the government and in turn private sector will provide health information and reporting to districts and regions. However, much work is still needed to improve outreach, collaboration, support, and regulation with the private sector, and there is no formal platform to share national malaria guidelines or best practices.

Progress since PMI was launched

In line with Ethiopia's long-standing policy that all patients with suspected malaria should receive a confirmatory diagnostic test before treatment with an antimalarial is prescribed, the FMOH has scaled up quality-assured diagnostic testing at both health facility and community level with support from PMI and the Global Fund. An analysis of micro-plan data indicates that Ethiopia has made significant progress in scaling-up diagnostic testing for malaria: the percentage of all suspected malaria cases reported that were diagnostically confirmed by either a RDT or microscopy increased from 59% in 2011 to 97% in 2014, leaving only 299,241 presumed malaria cases (i.e., "clinically treated" who were treated for malaria without laboratory confirmation). Figure 5 shows the rapid progress in malaria confirmatory testing in Ethiopia. In Oromia Region, confirmatory testing has increased from 67% in 2011 to 99% in 2014.

Figure 5: Trends in proportion of malaria cases tested with RDT or microscopy from 2011-2014 (EFY 2003-2006), by region (micro-plan data)

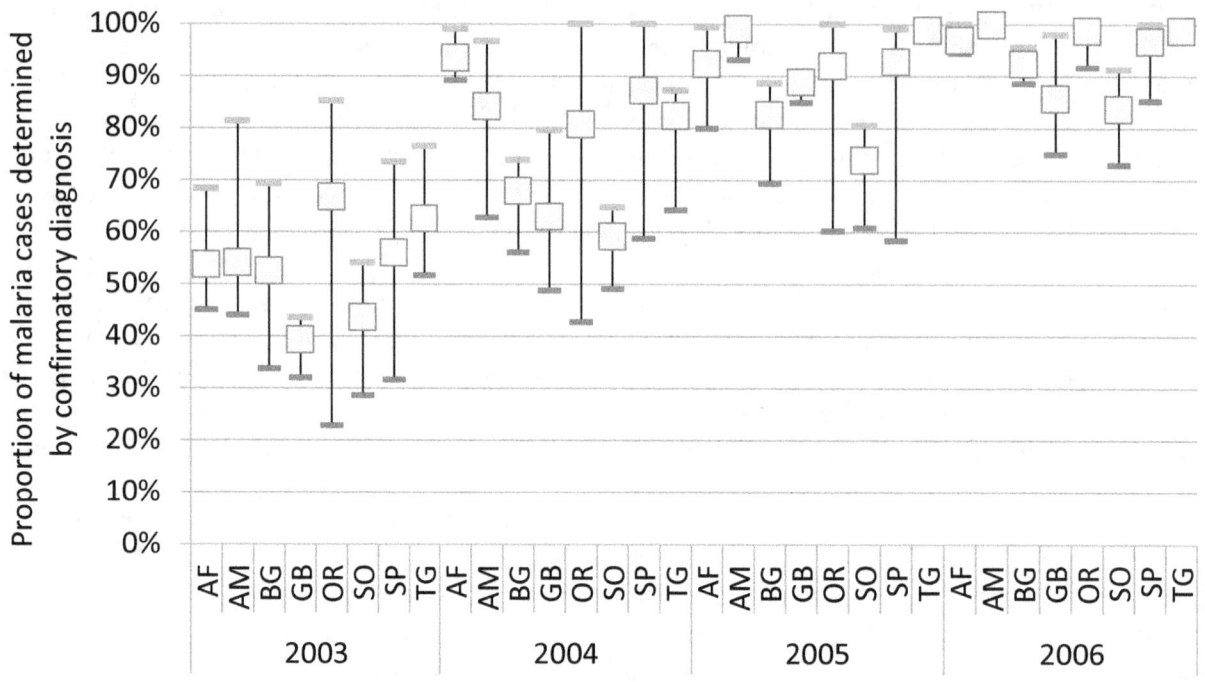

From FY 2008 through FY 2014, PMI procured 3.2 million RDTs, and 11.9 million ACT treatments, 153,000 artesunate suppositories, and 336,000 artesunate injections. The Global Fund and MDG pooled funds have also provided adequate quantities of ACTs and RDTs for the malaria program at the national level based upon recently strengthened surveillance and micro-plan reporting, although focal stockouts and drug expiry issues still exist.

In order to achieve NMSP targets of universal coverage of quality diagnosis at health centers, PMI has supported procurement of 621 microscopes, laboratory supplies, and reagents, to scale up quality assurance systems for malaria microscopy. PMI also supported the training of 2,253 workers in malaria microscopy and 18,316 health workers in the use of ACTs, as well as providing supervision of HEWs management of the sick child through iCCM, including performance of RDTs for managing acute febrile illnesses.

To date, PMI-supported quality assurance (QA) and quality control (QC) activities have largely been focused on microscopy in health centers, regional reference laboratories and hospitals, including supportive supervision of microscopy and RDT testing processes to minimize common errors. PMI has focused more on microscopy QA as the Global Fund has been primarily procuring RDTs for the past three years. The RDT QA/QC activities have been led by EPHI, which also has the capacity to conduct lot quality testing. In addition, Ethiopia participated in a pilot assessment of dried tube specimens for assessing RDT performance. While this has shown promising results, PMI is not currently pursuing this and will continue to monitor the development of positive control wells to improve RDT QC in the future.

PMI has supported private-public partnerships in collaboration with PEPFAR, one of the first attempts to understand private sector practices and challenges in Ethiopia, in order to improve private sector case management of malaria. Working together with the regional health bureaus and 83 private health facilities in four regional states, including Oromia Regional State, PMI supported increased access to quality malaria services, including diagnostic testing and free antimalarial treatment to the clients in the private sector.

Progress during the last 12-18 months

The FMOH's November 2014 annual review meeting report, which reported on PHEM data (July 2013-June 2014), stated that "out of the total 2,627,182 malaria cases reported 2,210,298 (84.1%) were confirmed by either microscopy or RDT, out of which 1,415,150 (64.0%) were *P. falciparum* and 795,148 (36.0%) were *P. vivax*." Although there are some differences in completeness and representativeness of these surveillance data, it is evident that the majority of malaria cases are now being laboratory confirmed, while surveillance systems continue to improve.

PMI supported in-service training of 1,952 HEWs for integrated malaria case management to ensure that malaria-specific updates for technical materials and guidelines are provided to USG-supported HEW training and capacity building programs, including MCH-funded activities. In 2014, PMI supported several rounds of microscopy training complemented by onsite supportive supervision and mentorship. PMI currently supports training and supervision of malaria diagnosis in 599 health centers with laboratories in malarious areas in Oromia. In FY 2015, PMI supported several laboratory strengthening activities for malaria microscopy including quality improvement, and purchasing laboratory equipment and additional supplies, supportive supervisions for treatment processes, and projects to improve private sector case management.

In order to reach more health facilities, PMI has built the capacity of EPHI to establish a national malaria slide archive, which will be used for training as well as proficiency testing. Through FY 2014, 1,503 standard slides have been produced. In addition, capacity of seven regional laboratories was built in five additional regional states to conduct cascade training and supervision of peripheral laboratories. PMI has provided technical and logistic support to ORHB to deliver integrated supportive supervision for malaria, HIV, and tuberculosis to an additional 130 health facilities currently not supported by PMI. PMI also leverages resources to conduct supportive supervision of HEWs through iCCM from other health programs.

In addition, PMI has supported the training of 654 laboratory personnel on an integrated malaria-HIV laboratory diagnosis and QA/QC system. Furthermore, 21 laboratory supervisors from regional reference laboratories have received training of trainers from all regional states. These supervisors are now planning to cascade basic trainings in all regional states of Ethiopia using funds from GoE and technical assistance from PMI. To improve the pre-service training of laboratory professionals and medical students on malaria diagnosis and treatment, training was provided to 30 university instructors from 8 major universities.

During the past 12 months, 234 health facilities were involved in an external QA scheme, and among those 76 facilities are involved in blind rechecking. It has been recognized that there is insufficient human and financial resources to support blinded rechecking of blood slides for all health facilities at regional reference laboratories. Therefore, facilities that score greater than 90% slide reading agreement with the regional reference laboratory on three successive rounds of rechecking will be considered "graduated" so that additional facilities can then undergo rechecking. To date, 134 health facilities have graduated.

Progress has been made in expanding supportive supervision to more health facilities in Oromia regional state, with 85% of the facilities (599/706) in malarious areas having received support. In addition, PMI will work to assist regional states to strengthen sub-regional reference laboratories and support hospital laboratory staff to supervise nearby facilities that are not currently receiving supportive supervision. In Ethiopia there are 3,245 health centers and 127 hospitals with microscopy diagnostic capacity, of which 75% of the facilities are in malarious areas. The large number of health facilities has posed challenges to scaling up external quality assurance to all facilities, as it requires skilled human resources and logistics to reach all facilities. In addition there are gaps in timely supply of quality reagents and laboratory supplies and maintenance of microscopes and laboratory equipment.

With FY 2015 funds, 154 private for-profit health facilitates will be supported to provide quality malaria case management. The facilities are estimated to diagnose about 544,000 suspected cases and treat over 109,000 confirmed cases. PMI will also support updating maps of workplace clinics that provide services to clients at the small and large scale farms and factories in malarious areas. About 22 such establishments will be supported in Amhara, Oromia, Tigray, SNNPR, Benishangul Gumuz, Afar and Gambela Regions to increase access to quality malaria services, including diagnostic testing and free antimalarial treatment to the clients in the private sector. These work place clinics are expected to diagnose more than 60,000 suspected cases and treat approximately 10,000 confirmed cases annually.

Commodity gap analysis

Table 8: RDT Gap Analysis

Calendar Year			
RDT Needs			
Target population at risk for malaria (*per Central statistics Agency, 2.6% growth rate*)	59,247,046	60,787,469	62,367,943
Total number projected fever cases**(*Micro-plan data - 2013/14 adjusting for underreporting*)	10,665,023	10,665,023	10,665,023
Percent of fever cases confirmed with microscopy	53%	53%	53%
Percent of fever cases confirmed with RDT	47%	47%	47%
Total RDT Needs (*Per Micro-plan data*)	12,102,764	12,102,764	12,102,764
Partner Contributions			
RDTs carried over (deficit) from previous year	4,412,290	860,776	2,807,186
RDTs from MOH	0	0	0
RDTs from Global Fund	8,551,250	8,460,939	7,243,576
RDTs from Other Donors	0	0	0
RDTs planned with PMI funding	0	5,588,235	2,900,000
Total RDTs Available	12,963,540	14,909,950	12,950,762
Total RDT Surplus (Gap)	860,776	2,807,186	847,998

Source: Micro plan data prepared January 2015
*fever cases are assumed to remain constant but procurement will be adjusted based on PFSA stock status and future micro-plan data
** the estimate factored unreported negative RDT results

Table 9: ACT Gap Analysis

Calendar Year	2015	2016	2017
ACT Needs			
Target population at risk for malaria *(per Central statistics Agency and the out years are multiplied by 2.6% growth rate)*	59,247,046	60,787,469	62,367,943
Total projected number of *P. falciparum* malaria cases *(per Micro plan data)*	2,331,491	2,069,220	1,742,501
Total ACT Needs	**2,956,516***	**2,881,109**	**2,426,197**
Partner Contributions			
ACTs carried over (deficit) from previous year	0	2,097,764	3,008,745
ACTs from MOH	0	0	0
ACTs from Global Fund	2,054,280	3,792,090	2,523,600
ACTs from Other Donors	0	0	0
ACTs planned with PMI funding	3,000,000	0	0
Total ACTs Available	5,054,280	5,889,854	5,532,345
Total ACT Surplus (Gap)	2,097,764	3,008,745	3,106,148

Note: *per micro plan 2015 data that include adjustment factor for using previous year data and 15% contingency; Projected *P. falciparum* cases for 2016 and 2017 are derived from FMOH's NMSP (2014-2020) goal of reducing cases by 75% from the baseline of 2013 (per micro-plan data)

Plans and justification

PMI plans to regularly reassess the commodity availability and distribution using data and information gathered from various sources (e.g., the Integrated Pharmaceutical Logistics System and micro-plan) and monitor the procurement and distribution of commodities through established malaria commodity technical working group. The commodity gaps identified and not covered by the Global Fund and MDG funds may be provided by PMI.

PMI will continue HEWs and health worker training/mentoring and supportive supervision to ensure early laboratory diagnosis and prompt treatment of all reported and confirmed malaria cases. The priority will be given to the HEWs working in remote hard-to-reach malarious areas especially in development areas. HEW training will be conducted as part of iCCM and specific training for clinicians will be conducted at regional levels.

Emerging data from episodic outbreak investigations and available epidemiological reports from routine surveillance suggest that older boys and men may now have special risks for malaria transmission from occupational and travel-related activities such as performing seasonal internal migrant farm work. Therefore, in addition to current private sector support for health facilities and clinics, PMI will continue to work with the FMOH, RHBs and private sector employers. PMI plans to support an assessment of prevention and control strategies for migratory workers especially in western part of the country where sesame farms and traditional gold mining are prevalent.

The FMOH recognizes that PMI provides a comprehensive and robust QA/QC system support for malaria laboratories and has requested that PMI support the introduction of microscopy QA/QC in at least one health center in each district. Building on lessons learned, the districts and regions may scale up to other health facilities. PMI envisions scaling up this support to all 706 facilities in Oromia by 2017. Outside of Oromia Regional State, PMI also plans to provide enhanced facility-based supportive supervisions to 162, 94, 41, and 16 health centers in Amhara, SNNP, Tigray, and Dire Dawa Regional States, out of 784, 572, 165, and 17 facilities, respectively.

The total number of health facilities (health centers and hospitals) in malarious areas of Ethiopia is 2,454. To date PMI has procured 621 microscopes that were provided to 513 health facilities (health centers and hospitals); of the remainder 100 were provided to the national reference laboratory and 8 to regional reference laboratories, where select microscopes were used to support training and EQA activities. PMI will procure an additional 207 microscopes using FY 2015 funds and another 207 using FY 2016 funds to cover 460 additional facilities that are being or will be enrolled in the EQA program in 2015 and 2016. In total, PMI will provide 927 microscopes, one for each health facility, by the end of 2017 (i.e., 38% of health facilities in malarious areas nationally). The procurement of microscopes is based on a facility assessment that will be conducted once the facilities are selected by the regional health bureaus.

PMI will build capacity of EPHI and regional reference laboratories to repair microscopes already in facilities. To promote standardization, PMI tries to ensure that malaria microscopes have similar formats and capabilities and will provide limited number of microscopes, spare parts, critical supplies, and reagents for malaria microscopy.

Proposed activities with FY 2016 funding: **($7,766,000)**

- **Procurement of RDTs ($1,884,000):** PMI will procure and distribute 2.9 million multi-species RDTs mostly to health posts. This will support the projected needs of the country.

- **Procurement of laboratory equipment/supplies ($400,000):** PMI will support procurement of approximately 207 microscopes and laboratory kits and spare parts to laboratories that conduct malaria microscopy. In addition, EPHI's biomedical maintenance capacity will be strengthened.

- **Support for QA system for malaria laboratory diagnosis ($500,000):** Under the current implementing mechanism, technical and programmatic support to health facility laboratories will be scaled up to more than 700 facilities in Oromia and to more than 300 health centers in other regional states mainly targeting high burden and malaria pre-elimination districts. Additionally, operational support will be provided to all regional reference laboratories in Ethiopia as well as major regional hospitals. This will include support for refresher training, supervision, other QA/QC activities, and program monitoring. Training and accreditation will be provided to laboratory supervisors.

- **Support for QA system for malaria laboratory diagnosis ($1,200,000):** The above activities will be scaled up under a new mechanism and similar technical and programmatic support will be provided to additional health facility laboratories in Oromia and other regional states targeting high burden and malaria pre-elimination districts.

- **Procurement of antimalarials for *P.vivax* treatment ($460,000):** PMI will support the procurement and distribution of the entire estimated national need for chloroquine and primaquine (i.e., 1.1 million treatments).

- **Procurement of pre-referral and severe malaria drugs ($822,000):** PMI will support the procurement and distribution of pre-referral drugs (i.e., rectal artesunate 20,000 vials), drugs for severe disease management (parenteral artesunate 300,000 vials and quinine IV 5,000 packs), and drugs for second-line treatment and pregnant women in their first trimester (quinine sulphate 1 million tablets), as needed.

- **Support for in-service training, supervision and monitoring of HEWs in providing malaria diagnosis and treatment ($1,700,000):** Support for supervision and monitoring of malaria treatment at primary healthcare units in Oromia, Amhara, SNNP, and Tigray Regional States will be continued. In addition, case management in the developing regions namely Gambela, Benishangul Gumuz, Somali and Afar will be supported. About 301 district health offices, 770 health centers, and more than 1,500 health posts will receive this support. More than 300 health workers, including HEWs, will receive in-service training in reviewing new malaria case management guidelines, on-site supervision, and ensuring that case management reporting is complete and accurate.

- **Private sector support to case management ($800,000):** PMI will work with the FMOH and RHBs to create an enabling policy and working environment for malaria prevention and control in private sector health services including the developmental areas in Oromia and Amhara Regions. PMI will provide technical assistance for planning, implementation, management and monitoring and evaluation of comprehensive malaria services to clients (formal and informal) at the private facilities, large farms and factories in malarious areas and increase access to quality malaria prevention and control services, including diagnostic testing and free antimalarial treatment to the clients in the private sector.

b. Pharmaceutical Management

NMCP/PMI objectives

The NMCP's goals of universal access to effective malaria case management requires best practices of pharmaceutical management and robust supply chains of malaria diagnostic and treatment commodities.

The FMOH and PMI have been working to address multiple supply chain problems within all levels of the national drug management system, including malaria commodity bottlenecks, stockouts, and expiry. In 2005, the FMOH developed a Pharmaceutical Logistics Management Plan and later in 2007 created the Pharmaceutical Funds Supply Agency (PFSA). Through mostly PEPFAR and Global Fund support, the FMOH radically redesigned the governance, policies, and infrastructure of the existing logistics system, establishing drug distribution regional hubs to directly supply health centers, health posts, and hospitals. Although PFSA began managing malaria commodities initially in 2011, the FMOH determined PFSA did not have the necessary capacity and issued a directive that all malaria procurements would be done by UNICEF and distributed through each of the regional health bureaus, leaving all other commodities (i.e., HIV, family planning, essential medicines, etc.) under the management of PFSA. During this time, PMI supported distribution of antimalarial medicines to the health facility level, primarily through the provision of technical assistance to regional health bureaus and health centers. As of November 2015, however, FMOH issued a new mandate requiring *all* commodities from all donors, including antimalarials, to be distributed through PFSA. The exception is for LLINs, which are distributed by UNICEF down to the district level. Once at the district level, LLINs are then distributed down to the household level through the HEP.

The Ethiopian Food Medicine Healthcare and Administration and Control Agency (FMHACA), organizationally under the FMOH, is responsible for regulating and registering medicines and ensuring the safety and quality monitoring of all medicines. It is also responsible for establishing and implementing QA systems for the country, including post-marketing drug quality monitoring, creating public awareness on quality assured medicines and taking legal and regulatory actions for fraudulent drugs.

Progress since PMI was launched

PMI has historically supported antimalarial drug management systems strengthening largely at hospital and health center levels. In addition PMI also supported PFSA and FMHACA in strengthening the pharmaceutical supply chain system, and antimalarial drug quality assessments, respectively.

In support of the antimalarial drug management system and pharmaceutical supply chain strengthening, PMI has been implementing several interventions in selected facilities. These interventions include anti-malaria drug management support through rational drug use, CRMS, supporting the establishment of Drug Therapeutic Committee, establishing Drug Information Centers and conducting end-use verification (EUV) surveys.

PMI has supported the strengthening of PFSA by seconding staff. PFSA is currently providing pharmaceutical service for the public and private health institutions through eleven regional-level hubs throughout Ethiopia. Until 2011, PMI has imported and distributed most of its malaria commodities (including ACTs) for Oromia Regional State through UNICEF. Since 2012 PMI has been procuring drugs including ACTs for national coverage and handing it over to PFSA for distribution.

With PMI support, micro-planning meetings with participants from all malaria-affected *woredas* and zones in Oromia Region were conducted annually since 2009 and in all regional states since 2011 to determine the requirements of ACTs, RDTs, and LLINs at the district level. The micro-plan is updated when distributions of commodities to the zones and districts occur. The ACT and RDT requirements were determined based on malaria cases diagnosed and treated from previous years at health facilities and health posts of each *woreda*. The results have subsequently been used to calculate the needs of pediatric and adult tablets of chloroquine to treat *P. vivax* malaria, and to prioritize and rationalize malaria commodity distributions through the year.

Micro-plans, while a very valuable annual activity, do not provide perfect estimates of resource and commodity requirements; specifically, they have not accounted for existing inventories or expiry dates of medicines or RDTs. Ultimately, in an epidemic-prone setting such as Ethiopia, redistribution of resources among or between districts may be needed to meet local needs that could not have been accurately forecasted from available data. Such flexible redistribution plans or processes are typically not available. The PFSA has yet to develop the capacity to meet the dynamic demands of the malaria transmission season or to respond promptly to urgent malaria medication stockouts. Some malaria commodities cost substantially less when ordered six or more months in advance, and some commodities have expiry dates of only two years; these factors create additional costs and increase the risk of waste particularly when logistics systems have slow procurement and customs clearance processes; slow, infrequent, and inflexible delivery cycles; and are unable to redistribute resources in the periphery based upon current malaria caseloads from one year to the next and even from season to season.

PMI-funded pharmaceutical facility baseline assessment surveys and ongoing reports reveal continued supply chain problems for malaria drugs in all regional states. There continue to be focal shortages and stockouts of ACTs (especially pediatric doses) and chloroquine, expired drugs and near-expiring RDTs, weak inventory control tools, inadequate medication records, and poorly organized and inadequate storage facilities.

Progress during the last 12-18 months

PMI supported PFSA by embedding qualified personnel through funded partners within their facilities, and providing resources for the development of standard operating procedures and forms for the quantification, requisition, drug exchange/transfer, and management of malaria commodities. In addition, PMI has improved malaria commodity management in 190 public health facilities (114 in Oromia and 76 in other Regional States). These included health centers improved through training and supportive supervision. With request from ORHB, malaria drug management data is now reported to the ORHB bi-monthly for 52 of these facilities in Oromia, including data on availability and expiry of antimalarial drugs, staff availability and capacity, and accurate reporting of antimalarial drug consumption. The data allows for monitoring and tracking of PMI- and ORHB-supported distribution of malaria commodities to health facilities and re-distribution of over-stocked drugs to districts with pending stockouts or shortages.

In support of the FMHACA, PMI conducted a rapid assessment of six regional FMHACA laboratories to strengthen post-marketing drug quality monitoring. Currently all compendial tests are conducted at the central laboratory. PMI plans to decentralize the capacity to regional laboratories. In FY 2014, the fifth round of drug sampling and laboratory confirmatory testing was completed. The results indicated that of the total 285 antimalarial samples subjected to compendial testing, only one sample of chloroquine (CQ) injection failed to comply with assay test. In addition, the surveillance has revealed that registration status of available antimalarial drugs has improved slightly from to 41% in 2013 to 66.7% in 2014.

In 2014, PMI expanded the post-market drug quality monitoring program to include four out of six regional FMHACA branch laboratories and further improved the regulatory capabilities of FMHACA. PMI also ensured that the activities are coordinated with other USG implementing partners and in-country stakeholders in a context of a changing Pharmaceutical Logistics Management Plan and the nascent establishment of the PFSA. Additionally, through support from PMI and PEPFAR, the national reference laboratory under FMHACA achieved ISO-17025 accreditation, demonstrating a higher level of quality including employment of standard operating procedures and an overall laboratory quality system. ISO certification enables the laboratory to conduct various analytical pharmacopeial testing procedures for human drugs.

With FY 2015 funding, PMI will continue to support FMOH and all regional states in Ethiopia in this micro-planning process for malaria commodities that is now recognized as a best practice. In the near future, there is a plan to investigate opportunities of integrating micro-planning with PHEM, HMIS, and Health Commodity Management Information System, for improved data capturing for decision making in the malaria control program.

PMI will continue to support PFSA particularly as the decision was made by FMOH at the end of last year to re-incorporate the management of malaria commodities through PFSA, transitioning the management from the regional health bureaus. As an interruption in the flow of malaria commodities cannot occur, PMI is supporting several implementing partners to provide significant technical assistance over the next 12 months.

PMI supported strengthening drug quality and safety monitoring capacities at FMHACA via post-marketing surveillance activities including use of Minilabs®. The Minilabs® are used to collect drug samples and provide preliminary field testing on quality of sampled medicines at customs check points, airports, and border ports of entry. Currently, there are seven sampling sites.

Plans and justification

The emerging capacities of PFSA and FMHACA provide an opportunity to assume more responsibility for pharmacy supply chains and antimalarial drug quality monitoring in the future, respectively. Strengthening pharmaceutical and malaria commodity supply chains will be a long term PMI investment. The micro-planning process has been recognized as a best practice in Ethiopia. Strengthening antimalarial drug management will also be needed throughout Ethiopia through a closer working relationship with PFSA. There will be an ongoing need to ensure quality of antimalarial drugs in Ethiopia to support quality malaria care and treatment in partnership with FMHACA.

Proposed activities with FY 2016 funding: **($1,900,000)**

- **Strengthening of antimalarial drug management ($1,000,000):** PMI will help sustain and expand the malaria drug management program from the current approximately 200 health centers covering approximately two-thirds of the malaria risk areas within Oromia Region, to support strengthening health systems and pharmacy logistics for PFSA-selected sites in all regional states of Ethiopia. The program will continue to focus on: improving the management of malaria commodities, including quantification, forecasting, requisition, drug exchange/transfer, and expiry tracking/disposal of various medicines. Specifically, focused activities will include:

- o improving overall drug management within health facilities and zonal/districts, resulting in improved commodities security and more robust pharmaceutical management capacity.
- o promoting the rational use of malaria drugs by training of PFSA and health facility level staff in drug management, as well as through on-site supportive supervision.
- o supporting data collection in selected facilities for CRMS.
- o improving access to good quality antimalarials through implementation of the PMI end-use verification survey.
- o implementing the Auditable Pharmaceutical Transaction System in selected health facilities in Oromia Regional state. Auditable Pharmaceutical Transaction System is service delivery arrangement to facilitate a transparent and accountable medicines transaction and service provision system at health facilities.

- **Strengthening PFSA pharmaceutical management capacities ($400,000):** PMI will provide support to PFSA to coordinate and design the best approach to integrating malaria commodities into the Integrated Pharmaceutical Logistics System. In addition, PMI will support improving malaria commodities quantification, requisition, drug exchange/transfer, and expiry tracking/disposal. PFSA's capacity will also be built to procure, prepare, and distribute quality reagents such as Giemsa solution for malaria diagnosis.

- **Strengthening drug quality monitoring ($500,000):** PMI will continue to strengthen FMHACA's drug quality assurance program by:
  - o supporting post-market drug quality monitoring in eight collection sites in all regional states.
  - o training FMHACA staff centrally and at the five regional laboratories on quality control testing of antimalarials.
  - o strengthening the GoE's central and regional quality control laboratories through training, technical assistance, sample collection, supportive supervision, and supply of equipment and reagents to FMHACA laboratories.
  - o strengthening regional regulatory offices that are responsible for regulating the retail drug outlets such as pharmacies and drug stores.
  - o conducting public awareness on fraudulent anti-malarials.
  - o improving data use and subsequent policy and regulatory measures.

- **Micro-planning surveys for estimating annual requirements and for assisting with distributions of malaria commodities (see M&E section):** With FY 2016 funding, PMI will continue to support FMOH through micro-planning meetings with participants from all malaria-affected *woredas* and zones in Ethiopia to determine the requirements of ACT treatments, RDTs, and LLINs at the district level. PMI supported micro plan activities will be increasingly integrated with and harmonized with PFSA and FMOH's *woreda*-based planning activities in the future.

5. Health system strengthening and capacity building

PMI supports a broad array of health system strengthening activities which cut across intervention areas, such as training of health workers, supply chain management and health information systems strengthening, drug quality monitoring, and NMCP capacity building.

NMCP/PMI objectives

The FMOH's NMSP (2014-2014) envisions a strengthened health system including well-trained human resources for health to support malaria control efforts nationwide. It also recognizes insufficient technical support and capacity building as well as shortages of human resources and turnover of experienced staff as major weaknesses in the health system of Ethiopia. The HEP has trained over 38,000 HEWs based at health posts, and these are assisted by many thousands of local volunteers within the HDA that together address many of the malaria health needs of their rural communities; the HDA workers typically focus on SBCC activities.

Ethiopia faces many challenges related to human resources for health service delivery, including the shortage of skilled health workers, high turnover, and lack retention of health professionals in remote and inaccessible health facilities where malaria is prevalent. Despite PMI and other donors' support, the NMCP has limited capacity in human resources and has not been able to effectively coordinate with PMI implementing partners and other partners in their many malaria-related activities. The high turnover rate at the FMOH and limited human resources capacities of RHBs are commonly mentioned as challenges for this effort. In addition, ORHB identified coordination of implementing partners as a major challenge. Decentralization of the health care system places an additional management burden on the Regional, Zonal, and District Health Offices.

Human Resource for Health is a five-year (2012-2017), USAID-funded bilateral program to support the efforts of the Ethiopian government in improving and retaining a skilled health workforce for service delivery of key health services including malaria. This program that involves both pre- and in-service trainings program has four key result areas:

- Improve HRH management
- Increase availability of midwives, anesthetists, HEWs, and other essential health workers
- Increase quality of health worker training
- Program learning and research

The FMOH has documented a shortage of malariologists and epidemiologists experienced in managing community-wide and very large-scale malaria epidemics and complex health emergencies. Ethiopia began its own FELTP, known locally as the EFETP, in October 2008 with technical assistance from CDC as a two-year, full-time, postgraduate competency-based training program consisting of about 25% class work and 75% field residency. The EFETP training is an in-service training program for PHEM health workers, who typically are already working (and continue to work) at zonal or regional health bureau offices. Trainees are closely supervised and provide epidemiologic service to the FMOH. Graduates of EFETP will receive a Master's Degree in Public Health and Field Epidemiology over a two-year training period. The program will join the African Field Epidemiology Network and work through the Ethiopian Public Health Association and EPHI. PMI has provided support to two EFETP residents annually since 2011 to enhance their training and expertise in malaria and related outbreaks of acute febrile illness that can be confused with malaria. The current PHEM surveillance system manager is a recent EFETP program graduate, as was the incident manager for recent Ebola preparedness activities in Ethiopia in 2014-2015.

Peace Corps Ethiopia

The U.S. Peace Corps has been active in Ethiopia for over fifty years with a few interruptions. The Peace Corps has provided many malaria-relevant activities and services over the years, including some educational programs for school-aged children and health promotion projects at the community level. Recently, PMI and Peace Corps developed a cooperative program entitled "Stomp Out Malaria," originally piloted by Peace Corps in Senegal. There are now over 100 Peace Corps volunteers in Ethiopia who have sufficient knowledge of malaria and of PMI's programs to help provide PMI-developed resources to HEWs and other district-level officials. They have also participated in World Malaria Day activities in Ethiopia. Peace Corps volunteers have helped to distribute LLIN distributions in some communities, and have helped to promote LLIN use through programs aimed at school-aged children.

Progress since PMI was launched

Through FY 2014, PMI cumulatively supported respective training for 19,949, 18,035, and 32,016 health workers in IRS operations, malaria diagnosis, and ACT treatments. As these trainings are part of a broader set of health systems strengthening activities, deliverables specific to malaria outcomes are not necessarily direct. Although this is a challenge, training inputs are primarily around strengthening various aspects of the health system. Ultimately, this will contribute to the development of a more competent and qualified workforce. The FMOH HRH strategy was released in June 2010. PMI has contributed through supporting pre- and in-service training for HEWs, midwives, and other healthcare workers, to include best practices in malaria diagnosis and treatment and prevention of malaria among pregnant mothers and newborns.

In 2011, three Ethiopian FELTP residents supported a comprehensive evaluation of PMI's ten epidemic detection sites. In late 2012, three FELTP residents participated (along with a CDC Epidemic Intelligence Service Officer) in a *P. vivax* therapeutic efficacy trial with chloroquine versus AL with or without primaquine after G6PD testing. Another FELTP resident has nearly completed a project that investigates the feasibility of using dried tube specimens of standard concentrations of previously laboratory-cultured *P. falciparum* as a reagent to assess the quality of malaria RDTs and the performance of health care workers in performing RDTs in field conditions (oral presentation at the ASTMH 2013 meeting). Another resident presented data at the Atlanta CDC Epidemic Intelligence Service conference in 2014 concerning a cluster of 10,000 acute febrile illnesses in an Ethiopia city that all tested negative by malaria laboratory tests, but was determined to be the first documented dengue fever outbreak in Ethiopia. Several other FELTP residents are finalizing protocols to investigate the epidemiology of malaria in various parts of Ethiopia or to evaluate malaria intervention coverage. In recent years, PMI has supported malaria related activities for a total of five EFETP trainees per year, with two or three from each of the two cohorts that are undergoing training.

Progress during the last 12-18 months

During 2015, PMI supported training of 2,860 midwives, 223 anesthetists, 2,033 HEW level IV, 2,659 HEW level III and 298 other essential health workers (emergency medical technicians and bio-medical technicians). Moreover, FMOH has been supported to develop the HRH strategic plan and draft policy and to train 754 managers at RHBs. Malaria case management training was provided for 25 instructors at Harar Regional Health Science College and malaria diagnosis and treatment curricula for 16 health education institutions was developed and distributed. Again, during this period refresher trainings have been provided to 50 HEWs' instructors. Similarly, the iCCM training module was developed for HEWs Level III.

Both the CDC Resident Advisor for EFETP and the PMI CDC Resident Advisor were involved in working with EFETP residents on Ebola Virus Disease preparations in Ethiopia and supporting international emergency responses while deployed to Liberia. The EFETP residents are producing a weekly analysis of PHEM data in respective districts, zones and regions, and are producing monthly and quarterly reports on an ongoing basis, thereby increasing epidemiological capacity and enhancing malaria control while strengthening health systems. The malaria focal person in the Amhara region who was a recent graduate of EFETP presented her ongoing analysis of Amhara region's recent PHEM malaria data during the MOP partners' meeting in May 2015 highlighting ongoing progress in malaria control and prevention.

The U.S. Peace Corps has been involved in a wide range of SBCC activities, including participation at World Malaria Day meetings. PMI provided 2,000 LLINs directly to Peace Corps for outreach activities in 2014 designed for static displays at youth camps to demonstrate proper use of LLINs at household level within communities at malaria risk.

Plans and justification

While it is beyond the ability of PMI to address the system-wide capacity issues, there are several areas within the NMCP and RHBs where capacity can be strengthened with PMI assistance, including through pre- and in-service refresher trainings. The health systems strengthening and capacity building activities supported by PMI are in line with the FMOH's strategies, and support remaining gaps in training and human resources. Nationally there is a need to develop the capacity of local NGOs working on health and specifically on malaria prevention and control. These local NGOs have some capacity in assisting the districts and HEWs in planning, implementing and monitoring malaria prevention and control related activities. Therefore, USAID/Ethiopia's Health, AIDS, Population and Nutrition office is intending to engage with the consortium of local NGOs, operating throughout the country. PMI plans to conduct specific short term trainings for the NGOs in highly malarious areas, provide the necessary tools, and work with them to improve case management and LLIN utilization.

Proposed activities with FY 2016 funding: **($1,030,000)**

- **Coordination support for ORHB and NMCP ($250,000):** Support joint planning, coordination, supportive supervision, and review activities with all malaria stakeholders in ORHB and at national level.

- **Pre-service training of HEWs ($300,000):** As a major nationwide health program, HEP requires substantial investment in human resources, health infrastructure, and provision of equipment, supplies and commodities, as well as other operating costs. The pre-service training of HEW is a one-year training which includes coursework as well as field work to gain practical experience. HEWs carry out and promote 16 preventive health actions in which malaria prevention and control is one of the actions.

- **Field Epidemiology and Laboratory Training Program ($250,000):** PMI will continue to support three to five EFETP residents to support human resources for health development among epidemiologists and to strengthen the PHEM epidemic detection system and malaria surveillance including weekly bulletins.

- **Malaria prevention activities by Peace Corps ($30,000):** PMI will support two Peace Corps volunteers (PCVs) and provide small grants for malaria projects to strengthen the community level malaria prevention activities working with HEWs in hard-to-reach areas such as Gambella and Benishangul Gumuz. Malaria-focused PCV field activities in remote settings include: training teachers, school children, and community mobilizers and conduct community-based SBCC activities in collaboration with HEWs on LLINs use, improving early treatment-seeking and treatment compliance.

- **Local NGO empowerment ($200,000):** PMI will strengthen the capacity of local NGOs that operate in malaria endemic areas to conduct malaria control and prevention activities with an emphasis on LLIN promotion and malaria case management.

6. Social and behavior change communication (SBCC)

NMCP/PMI objectives

The importance of prevention, health promotion and SBCC were highlighted in the previous Ethiopian HSDPs and will remain a priority in the new HSTP 2016-2020. The Ethiopian DHS 2011 showed that the level of exposure to mass media is low in Ethiopia. Only 22% of women and 38% of men listened to the radio at least once a week. In addition, 68% of women aged 15-49 and 54% of men in the same age group did not have access to any of the three common media types (TV, radio, or print). Nationally, progress has been observed in terms of LLINs use among children under five in households that owned LLINs. According to the MIS 2011, the percentage of children under five in households that owned LLIN and who had slept under a LLIN the previous night was 60% in 2007, increasing to 65% in 2011. Tigray Region demonstrated the greatest increase, with 47% in 2007 to 68% in 2011. Oromia Region showed a decrease in LLIN use by children under five to 55%. National findings showed no improvement in LLIN use among pregnant women in 2011 compared to 2007. SNNPR demonstrated the highest improvement in LLIN use among pregnant women from 63% in 2007 to 75% in 2011.

The SBCC's role in achieving NMCP objectives in malaria control across interventions is clearly stated in the NMSP 2014–2020. The SBCC objective in the NMSP states: "By 2020, all households living in malaria endemic areas will have the knowledge, attitudes and practices towards malaria prevention and control." In achieving this objective, the NMSP focused on utilization of HEWs, with the support of HDAs and model family households. Despite the absence of a malaria-specific communication strategy, the national health communication strategy launched in 2004 provides a guide for all areas of health including malaria prevention and control. This strategy document is currently under revision and will give details of malaria communication approaches and implementation at various levels.

According to the new NMSP, the strategies for community empowerment and mobilization include:
- conducting integrated refresher training on malaria SBCC for HEWs
- developing and integrating the malaria communication strategy into the national communication strategy
- increasing the use of supportive mass media
- integrating malaria prevention and control into school programs
- conducting advocacy to gain strong commitment of the local leaders in malaria elimination districts
- producing and distributing IEC/ BCC materials
- conducting orientation workshops for HDAs on community mobilization including iCCM service and its importance
- conducting formative research on knowledge, attitudes, and practices

Social behavior change communication activities through mass media and rural communications campaigns and supporting community-level change agents like HDAs, religious leaders and school children can be applied in an integrated fashion for the malaria interventions (e.g., LLINs, IRS, early diagnosis and treatment compliance). For communications activities related to RDTs and ACTs in particular, PMI will work with health providers at different levels of the health system to strengthen their interpersonal communication skills. The SBCC strategy may follow any behavioral framework that is appropriate for the Ethiopia situation. An example of a framework that may offer a way to organize the SBCC approach is the so-called "Essential Malaria Actions" which will also supplement the SBCC activities of HDAs and HEWs.

Progress since PMI was launched

Since 2009, PMI has provided assistance to the FMOH to carry out malaria-related SBCC activities. Working with the regional, zonal, and district offices as well as HEP, including HDAs, PMI has delivered critical SBCC activities. In the past, PMI's support to the FMOH primarily focused on increasing demand for LLINs and improving correct, consistent and sustained use of LLINs as well as improving treatment seeking behavior and increasing community awareness about malaria and its prevention and control. Additionally, PMI increased the awareness in the community about the effectiveness of IRS in order to reduce refusal of IRS or re-plastering of sprayed walls.

The target audiences were all community members in project areas and specific attention was given to schools and teachers and enabling students to act as change agents for educating family members and neighbors. In addition, SBCC activities were focused on pregnant women who visited health facilities for ANC. Several communication channels like mass media (community radios), interpersonal communication (IPC), health education at facilities, family folders with malaria messages at the household level, SBCC campaigns and mass mobilization through schools were utilized.

The malaria messages were very focused, clear, and actionable. If a family completed the four malaria "doable actions" related to LLINs use, prompt treatment seeking, completion of malaria medication, and IRS, a *Family Health Sticker* was placed on the entry door, recognizing it as a model family for health.

Through PMI's earlier support to SBCC, net utilization among pregnant women increased from 21% at baseline to 54% at end line and use by children under five years of age increased from 26% to 54%. The number of households accepting IRS increased from 39% in 2009 to 58% in 2012. In Oromia caregivers who sought treatment for their children under five years of age rose from 54 to 57%. Eighty percent of respondents reported that malaria is a preventable disease, 74% knew LLINs provided protection against malaria infection, 63% were aware that malaria was transmitted through a mosquito bite, and 87% acknowledged the importance of children under five years of age seeking prompt treatment. Generally, there were significant improvements in malaria prevention and control knowledge in the project communities. This effort in SBCC was complemented by hang-up campaigns in collaboration with the U.S. military that targeted the most vulnerable groups, i.e., pregnant women and children under five years of age. Increasing community awareness about the effectiveness of IRS, improving treatment-seeking behavior for malaria (e.g., timeliness, appropriateness) and increasing community knowledge regarding malaria diagnosis, treatment, prevention, and control were also among the major priorities.

During 2014, PMI/Ethiopia initiated and supported two local organizations' community-based malaria SBCC activities, as part of the USAID/Ethiopia Local Capacity Development program. These community-based malaria SBCC activities are being implemented in selected zones of Oromia and Amhara Regions for a three-year period (2014-2016). These project activities were intended to complement and support the national malaria SBCC activities through capacity building of selected schools and faith-based organizations (FBOs) in high malaria transmission areas. The project uses harmonized malaria messages (eight essential malaria actions and four do-able actions) developed by PMI and conducts SBCC-related activities in coordination with HEWs.

Progress during the last 12-18 months

During FY 2015, PMI has been implementing malaria SBCC activities in 5 districts, 125 primary schools and 128 churches in 123 *kebeles* in Amhara Region. During the last 12 months, 125 (100%) targeted malaria school clubs were provided with school mini-media equipment to disseminate malaria messages to school communities. In order to reach school and local communities with Essential Malaria Actions messages 2,024 peer education leaders were trained; these leaders reached 22,000 students, and these students in turn educated their families at home. Through various mass campaign events, nearly 13,000 community members were reached in the 123 *kebeles*. Malaria basic training was given to 609 focal persons from schools, religious institutions, and communities. Progress also included the production and dissemination of 2,750 peer education to 125/125 (100%) targeted schools along with the distribution of 20,000 IEC/SBCC pieces, which included leaflets, posters, and banners.

PMI supported SBCC activities in Oromia Region, which focused on building local capacities of schools and religious institutions to conduct SBCC activities targeting malaria prevention and control interventions. During the last 12 months, malaria SBCC was implemented in 90/145 (62%) of the targeted schools, in 83 health posts, 48 mosques, and 33 churches. Schools were equipped with mini-media materials to build the capacity of the established 41 anti-malaria clubs.

Both projects are reproducing the PMI-developed IEC/SBCC materials which contain standardized and harmonized malaria messages adapted to local situations. Unsurprisingly, limited project and financial management capacity was one of the challenges in supporting local organizations. In order to tackle build management capacity, USAID/Ethiopia engaged a contractor to build capacity of these local organizations specifically on project and financial management.

Plans and justification

PMI will continue to support SBCC activities focusing on affected communities in high malaria transmission districts (157 districts) to complement and support the national malaria SBCC strategies. In addition, very specific and targeted SBCC activities in low transmission areas will be carried out to encourage early diagnosis and prompt treatment as well as sustaining LLIN utilization. The pre-elimination districts and the specific malaria activities and interventions that will be unique to these districts have not yet been defined by the FMOH. PMI will work to incorporate pre-elimination specific behavioral interventions based on the identified risk factors once these activities and strategies are developed by the FMOH with input from PMI. PMI also will recommend the use of international best practices, validated tools, and experiences from other countries on elimination-related behavioral interventions.

The proposed activities with FY 2016 funding will support and reinforce interpersonal communication channels to deliver malaria messages and work through a wide range of implementing partners and in-country stakeholders including HEWs and HDAs at the community level.

With FY 2016 funding, malaria SBCC activities will be more integrated and coordinated with other health SBCC activities for prevention of mother-to-child transmission of HIV, tuberculosis, family planning/reproductive health, MNCH, and nutrition. PMI will also continue to support local organizations through an Annual Program Statement mechanism to build local capacity in communicating malaria key messages through schools and FBOs.

PMI will provide capacity building and coordination support to the Health Education Team at the FMOH (central and regional level) and will review and harmonize the existing malaria SBCC tools and materials to deliver them through appropriate media channels based on evidence. Interpersonal communication as well as entertainment education, using schools, and religious institutions will be encouraged. Promotional efforts on early diagnosis and prompt treatment and consistent and proper LLIN use will be scaled up and will use alternative SBCC interventions to reach target groups with no access to radio and television. Suggested interventions include school programs and community meetings as well as other creative methods. Focus will be put on strategies initiated by the communities themselves, i.e., through HDAs. In this effort, PMI's community-based SBCC activities will complement and reinforce the government's community-based health communication initiative by mobilizing school and faith-based communities as change agents.

Proposed activities with FY 2016 funding: **($1,900,000)**

- **Coordination and capacity building for SBCC ($450,000):** With FY 2016 funding, PMI will build capacity within national and regional health bureaus, *woredas*, and Primary Health Care Units as well as local institutions, including NGOs, community-based organizations, and FBOs to coordinate, plan, manage, implement, and evaluate health SBCC programs and interventions. In addition, technical assistance will be provided to review/update SBCC messages, tools, and identify effective channels of communication for different epidemiological settings and target groups.

- **Community-based SBCC for LLINs, IRS, ACTs, case management ($1,050,000):** PMI will continue to support the implementation of evidence-based and coordinated SBCC activities at community level in malarious areas to increase the knowledge, attitudes, and practices towards malaria prevention and control, and to increase coverage and access to malaria services.

- **Community-based SBCC Oromia, Jimma Zone ($200,000):** With FY 2016 funding, PMI will continue to support a local University to carry out community based SBCC activities in selected ten *woredas* of Oromia Region. PMI will continue to target school communities, FBOs, and local media. This will help to reinforce and complement the HDAs community-based interpersonal behavioral change interventions.

- **Community-based SBCC Amhara Region ($200,000):** With FY 2016 funding, PMI will continue to support a local organization to carry out community based BCC activities in selected ten *woredas* of Amhara Region. PMI will continue to target school communities, FBOs, and local media. This will help to reinforce and complement the HDAs community-based interpersonal behavioral change interventions.

7. Monitoring and evaluation (M&E)

NMCP/PMI objectives

The FMOH's NMSP (2014-2020) highlights the need for ongoing M&E and emphasizes the constant need for detection and response to focal and widespread malaria epidemics. A new M&E plan to replace the previous 2010-2015 plan is currently being developed to reflect the new NMSP. The NMSP describes the M&E framework and its four key areas: 1) Monitoring the operational aspects of the program and measuring impact, outcome, or process indicators to ensure that the activities are yielding desired results and moving the program towards achieving its operational targets and objectives; 2) Monitoring changes in epidemiological indicators resulting from the activities implemented, 3) Appropriately interpreting results and informing revisions in policies or strategies, when needed, to help ensure progress; and 4) Documentation of progress towards malaria elimination. In addition to the malaria morbidity and mortality impact indicators, they have added elimination specific indicators to monitor the proportion of previously malarious *kebeles* reporting no monthly malaria cases for 24 months and number of w*oredas* with zero locally transmitted cases of malaria.

In 2009, the PHEM surveillance system was developed to cover the entire country, encompassing reporting from health posts, health centers, and hospitals. The PHEM aims to be a weekly multi-disease reporting system that collects a range of malaria indicators, mostly related to outpatient malaria morbidity. The PHEM surveillance reporting covered 83% of districts throughout Ethiopia as of 2013, aiming to provide weekly reports from all health facilities, including health posts, through district health offices. Functionally, though, most districts only provide monthly reports, and rural health post reporting has lagged behind most other facilities. The PHEM depends on accurate and timely information reported from HEWs and health facilities, therefore building capacity though the health post level is essential. Malaria cases are reported by two age groups (less than and more than five years of age) including clinical malaria (outpatient and inpatient), and confirmed malaria by species. Assuming that improved IRS coverage and LLIN use will continue to reduce malaria transmission, the focus of malaria control and elimination will increasingly turn towards enhancing surveillance with the aim of halting ongoing transmission, and to investigating all cases, and to prevent re-introduction of focal transmission in previously malaria-free areas.

Currently, Ethiopia has a paper-based system of data collection at the health facility level; however, these data have not always been optimally analyzed or used for decision-making and resource allocation at the local, regional, or national level. Consequently, Ethiopia's FMOH is in the process of revising the HMIS, while making some reporting electronic. This revised HMIS, which includes a total of 106 indicators and is primarily supported via funds from PEPFAR and the Global Alliance for Vaccines and Immunization, aims to provide one standardized set of health indicators nationally. Unfortunately, HMIS reports quarterly from health centers and hospitals at the district level (no data reporting from health post) and reports of these data are usually not published for one or two years after they are collected. The most relevant and accurate data contained in these reports are inpatient cases and malaria deaths, although over 83% of health facilities that are hospitals and health centers are reporting on outpatients cases as of 2014. As of 2015, outpatient malaria cases diagnosed at health posts are not included in HMIS morbidity reports as published in the annual Health and Health Related Indicators reports. There are only two malaria-specific indicators in the HMIS:

- Malaria cases reported per 1,000 population, disaggregated into clinical and confirmed cases, with the latter further disaggregated by species, i.e., *P. falciparum*/other, among:
  - children under five years of age, and
  - people at least five years of age; and

- Malaria case fatality rate among:
  - children under five years of age [inpatients]
  - people at least 5 years of age [inpatients]

Malaria epidemics in Ethiopia have been documented since the 1930s. A catastrophic malaria epidemic in 1958 was responsible for an estimated 3 million clinical cases of malaria and 150,000 malaria deaths. Since 1958, major epidemic years have occurred approximately every five to eight years (Tulu, A. N. "Malaria", In: Kloos, H. and Zein, A. Z., *The Ecology of Health and Disease in Ethiopia*, 1993, West

57

View Press Boulder, San Francisco, Oxford, pp. 341-352). Current methods for epidemic detection in Ethiopia rely on passive case detection of clinically diagnosed cases at health posts and health centers. In this system, the median weekly clinically diagnosed malaria cases over the previous five years are charted. Thresholds are set by either the third quartile (second highest number from the five previous years' data for that week) or double the previous year's number of cases in that week. If the number of cases in a given week exceeds the set threshold, the health worker is to report a potential epidemic. A rapid assessment team is then dispatched to confirm that an epidemic exists or is threatening, establish the cause and scale of the epidemic, and identify local capacity to respond. The guidelines recommend presumptive mass fever treatment with ACTs for fever cases if the test positivity rate is ≥ 50 percent. A stock of 15-20% of ACTs is to be held at the regional level for epidemic response. If there is potential for continued transmission, IRS will be implemented. For this reason, all districts with a potential for epidemics are advised to reserve a stock of insecticide for epidemic response and spraying operations would begin following either a three- or six-day training period for local spray operators.

Progress since PMI was launched

Since the launch of PMI, PMI has provided substantial support for M&E strengthening activities including support for large household surveys e.g., the MIS 2007, MIS 2011, and ongoing support for the planned 2015 survey, as well as strengthening routine surveillance systems.

PMI supports the PHEM system. This support has been targeted to enhance reporting from rural health posts where half of all malaria morbidity is detected and treated, and to enable reporting of more complete RBM-MERG indicators on a weekly basis. PMI had supported the collection of comprehensive, timely malaria surveillance data in ten sentinel districts. This support included data analysis, training and supervisory support.

PHEM and HMIS report to different directorates within FMOH, have separate staffing and reporting structures, and serve different functions. There are no plans to integrate them at this time. Reporting completeness has rapidly improved for both PHEM and HMIS. PHEM reporting completeness is now 83%, and HMIS completeness is 85-95%, not including health post data. The reported PHEM malaria totals will be nearly double compared to HMIS since it includes data from health posts which manages approximately half of the cases. The inpatient malaria totals should be consistent between these systems.

The annual micro-plan that surveys all malaria health officers within malarious districts has had 99% completeness of reporting in the last three years, offering the most comprehensive surveillance system available to supplement the PHEM and HMIS surveillance systems, however, it only occurs once a year. Although there are currently three separate sources of reported malaria cases and deaths (Table 10), the systems have differing attributes and coverage. Overall, all three systems reflect decreasing trends since 2011/2012 to the most recent 2013/2014 data. PHEM and HMIS report very similar malaria case data: approximately 3.4 million clinical and confirmed cases in 2011/2012 decreasing to 2.6 million cases in 2013/2014. Microplanning data reported 5,559,624 confirmed and clinical cases in 2011/2012 decreasing to 3,558,360 in 2013/2014. With improving coverage of PHEM and HMIS system, the differences in the annual reported number of malaria cases are decreasing. The team will continue to monitor these systems and trends.

Data from microplanning activities is used for quantification and forecasting antimalarial commodity needs, which is based on health facility level morbidity data for each district in malarious areas. These data are different from the data collected by the EUV tool. EUV data are collected at one point in time and in only a fraction of health facilities. The primary objective of EUV activities is to inform the PMI commodities team on general ACT and RDT availability at a regional level, on a real-time level. This helps avoid immediate stockouts, as it enables the PMI headquarters commodity team to mobilize both emergency commodity funds (i.e., for the procurement of needed commodities) and/or access to PMI's ACT buffer stock. A secondary objective of the EUV is to inform the relevant GoE stakeholders such as PFSA, about gross or systemic issues along the supply chain continuum, contributing to the technical support already provided by PMI's implementing supply chain partners. Therefore, there is both an immediate use of the data and a longer-term, health-system strengthening purpose.

Attributes of the various surveillance systems and data sources are provided in the following table:

Surveillance System	Reporting Frequency	Facilities Reporting	Publications	Comment
Health Management Information System (HMIS)	Quarterly	Hospitals, Health Centers	Annual (Health and Health-Related Indicators)	Most complete for inpatient malaria reporting and inpatient deaths; some stratification of data by gender and for children
Integrated Disease Surveillance System (IDSR)	Monthly	Hospitals, Health Centers	Annual (Health and Health Related Indicators, until 2009)	IDSR malaria data have not been reported since 2009: folded into PHEM
Public Health Emergency Management (PHEM) System	Weekly	Hospitals, Health Centers, and Health Posts	Annual (Annual Review Meeting Report, and World Malaria Report)	Timely, complete, designed for outbreak detection; began in 2009 building upon former IDSR system; PHEM is the primary data source for Annual Review Meeting and the WHO World Malaria Reports, and Global Fund 2014 NFM application
Micro-plan	Annual	Hospitals, Health Centers, Health Posts	Not for public distribution but used for programming	Began national reporting in 2010; Includes number of persons tested and suspected malaria (clinical plus tested malarias), includes commodities data, most complete available reporting as of 2013, not stratified by age or gender; data are reported and analyzed by district while accounting for component health facilities

Guidelines for malaria epidemic prevention and control were updated in 2012 with support of PMI and are available on the FMOH's website. For updates about the current status of malaria outbreaks in Ethiopia, see the Introduction and the Malaria Situation section within the Strategy. These new guidelines detail the human vulnerability factors, including population movement, as well as meteorological factors, such as rainfall, temperature, and humidity, that affect the occurrence of epidemics. The revised guidelines include setting detection thresholds at the health post level and strategies for mapping malaria micro-foci or micro-clusters.

Progress during the last 12-18 months

PMI has been coordinating surveillance strengthening efforts through the existing PHEM system. Over the past year rapid reporting systems to strengthen PHEM reporting of malaria cases from the health post to the health centers have been rolled out to ten districts in Oromia to strengthen malaria epidemic detection and response. PMI's experience with implementing rapid reporting to enable epidemic detection in Oromia and the lessons learned was recently published in a peer-reviewed journal (Yukich et. al., 2014).

With malaria elimination targets set for 50 districts by 2020, PMI has been providing technical assistance with drafting the elimination strategy, plans, and district selection process including refining the criteria and contributing data from the micro-plan. PMI and the FMOH co-sponsored a pre-elimination conference in May 2015 to share malaria activities and tactics that are relevant to pre-elimination both from Ethiopia and from several other countries including Sri Lanka, Senegal, and Zambia. In-depth discussions with local and international experts from WHO Global Malaria Program, MACEPA, and Global Fund addressed many technical and practical aspects of implementing malaria elimination e.g. human resource and capacity, surveillance systems, M&E plan, and case management and vector control needs which will be funded by the Global Fund NFM.

A MIS survey is scheduled to take place in Ethiopia in late 2015 with PMI financial and technical support. Molecular testing for common G6PD deficient variants from a random sub-set of the MIS 2011 dried blood spots revealed no A- or Med variants. Results of the serology testing of the MIS 2011 samples are not yet available due to major delays in procuring the needed laboratory supplies. LLIN durability monitoring began in mid-2015 coordinated with the mass distribution campaigns.

PMI supported an in vivo efficacy study that was completed after enrolling 399 patients in December 2014 for CQ or AL therapy with or without primaquine (PQ) to measure therapeutic efficacy in patients with *P. vivax* infection. Preliminary analyses revealed the efficacy rate at day 42 for CQ alone was 81.2%, following AL alone was 70%, following combined CQ+PQ was 98.8%, and following combined AL+PQ was 93.3%. The risk of recurrence at 12 months for CQ alone was 60%, for AL alone was 66.6%, for combined CQ+PQ was 20.5%, and for combined AL+PQ was 37.8%. These data suggest that broader use of PQ combination therapy should greatly reduce *P. vivax* recurrences within 42 day and one year follow up intervals.

An Ethiopian service provision assessment (SPA, or eSPA+) survey was completed in 2014 in Ethiopia (without PMI funding), and the FMOH drafted these preliminary findings: "Draft analysis of ESPA+ indicated that malaria diagnosis and/or treatment services are universally available in most of Ethiopian health facilities. More than 90% of health facilities excluding health posts (77% of health posts) offer malaria treatment services; however, a little less than 50% of these facilities have laboratory diagnostic capacity for malaria. Overall, 60% of health facilities excluding health posts have capacity for parasitological diagnosis of malaria using either microscopy or rapid diagnostic tests. About 85% of government facilities have the capacity to provide malaria diagnostics compared with 28% of private-for-profit facilities (draft eSPA+, 2014). About 42% of all facilities that provide malaria services had stock of first-line ACTs with 74% of the stocks are from government owned facilities and 4% stocks are from private-for-profit facilities."

Table 11: Monitoring and Evaluation Data Sources

Data Source		2010	2011	2012	2013	2014	2015	2016	2017	2018
National-level Household surveys	Demographic Health Survey (DHS)*		X				X			
	Malaria Indicator Survey (MIS)		X				X			X
	EPI survey*			X						
Health Facility and Other Surveys	School-based malaria survey		X	X	X					
	Health facility survey*		X							
	SPA survey*					X				
	EUV survey					X	X	X	X	
Malaria Surveillance and Routine System Support	Support to malaria surveillance system	X	X	X	X	X	X	X	X	X
	Support to Micro-plan	X	X	X	X	X	X	X	X	X
	Support to HMIS*									
Therapeutic Efficacy monitoring	Falciparum in vivo efficacy testing			X*				X		X
	Vivax in vivo efficacy testing			X	X	X		X		X
Entomology	Entomological surveillance and resistance monitoring	X	X	X	X	X	X	X	X	X
	LLIN durability monitoring						X	X	X	
Other malaria-related evaluations	Serology/G6PD surveys					X	X+			
Other Data Sources	Malaria Impact Evaluation					X	X			
*Not PMI-funded , + results pending										

Plans and justification

PMI will continue to strengthen PHEM reporting of malaria cases from the health post to the health centers in selected districts to strengthen malaria epidemic detection and response. PMI will continue to work with HEWs, HEW supervisors, and health workers to collect timely, quality surveillance data in selected districts to improve routine malaria surveillance systems and timely detection of epidemics and response. Quality assurance of data collection and capacity building of the HEWs will be facilitated by HEW supervisors who will receive HEW supervisor training to conduct integrated supervisions and regular field visits in 293 districts in 6 regional states (approximately one-third of the country).

PMI will continue supporting the national malaria commodities micro-planning exercise which gives a nearly complete picture of the national commodity needs. It is different from the PMI-funded EUV which is conducted in only 20 facilities quarterly (out of 3,000 health facilities in the country) and only collects data on stock availability of antimalarial drugs and RDTs. Micro-planning is a nationwide annual quantification of all malaria commodities including LLINs and is based on health facility level morbidity data for each district in malaria endemic areas. The micro-planning exercise has helped PMI, Global Fund, and the FMOH to quantify the country's total commodity needs (all antimalarials, RDTs, and LLINs) at the district level, and to plan commodity procurement and distribution. This is the only data source that provides over 97% completeness of data on commodity availability and need at the national level. It also provides comprehensive malaria morbidity data which can be triangulated to the HMIS and PHEM annual data.

With malaria elimination goals, PMI will continue to provide technical assistance and support to the FMOH in augmenting their surveillance and M&E systems to meet the specific programmatic needs to monitor elimination efforts. Building on the elimination conference in May 2015, PMI will continue to engage with the FMOH as they design a strategic approach and outline the specific activities that will be pursued in the elimination districts. PMI will continue to work closely with the FMOH to ensure that new elimination specific activities that will be undertaken with Global Fund support (e.g., the roll out of single dose PQ and reactive case detection activities) are adequately evaluated as to inform future strategies for Ethiopia and other countries pursuing elimination (see operational research section).

PMI will continue to support periodic household surveys to monitor national progress, continue drug efficacy tests on vivax malaria to complement Global Fund-supported falciparum efficacy studies and continue to monitor LLIN durability.

Proposed activities with FY 2016 funding: **($1,520,000)**

- **Strengthening PHEM system and epidemic response ($1,000,000):** Strengthening the PHEM system and improving reporting of malaria cases from the health post to the health centers and to strengthen malaria epidemic detection and response in hotspot districts nationally. PMI will support the FMOH, RHBs, and malaria pre-elimination districts to address data management capacity gaps to capture all malaria cases reported, compile them, analyze and prepare reports and use that information for programmatic purposes at regional, zonal, district and facility levels. Currently PMI is collaborating with EPHI to design a training and supportive supervision program that will be rolled-out to the districts and health facilities to capacitate surveillance officers to effectively collect, organize, analyze, and use malaria data for decisionmaking at all levels. This also includes reporting of outbreaks and epidemics if they occur in those facilities and districts.

- **National malaria commodities micro-plan ($350,000):** PMI will continue to support annual assessments of malaria commodity gaps and malaria morbidity from all malaria endemic districts (note: this activity is separate from the EUV; please see text above regarding use of data from EUV activities).

- **LLIN durability monitoring ($150,000):** Year 3 of LLIN durability monitoring. LLIN durability assessment at set intervals post distribution to determine if policies that assume LLINs are effective for three years are valid in the Ethiopian context.

- **M&E technical assistance ($20,000):** Two TDYs to provide technical assistance for surveillance, M&E activities including LLIN durability assessment.

8. Operational research (OR)

The FMOH's NMSP (2014-2020) envisions the need for operational research studies to guide program decisions. Some of the priority areas for OR include studies to detect insecticide and antimalarial drug resistance, and to improve the effectiveness of antimalarial interventions, while anticipating program needs related to pre-elimination activities. Priority areas for PMI Ethiopia OR are informed by the PMI strategy and the PMI OR priorities. NMCP research priorities come from National Malaria Strategic Plans. PMI has also sponsored various conferences involving universities and EPHI, the lead agency for medical research within FMOH, and partners to learn about ongoing research and to harmonize PMI Ethiopia's OR priorities with FMOH research goals. PMI, in conjunction with the FMOH, also supported a conference in May 2015 bringing together the FMOH, donors, WHO, NGOs, and other stakeholders to discuss plans to select the target elimination districts and the specific steps needed to achieve the goal of eliminating malaria from 50 districts by 2020. As Ethiopia embarks on implementing new elimination-specific strategies and policies (e.g., rolling out single dose primaquine for falciparum malaria, radical cure of vivax, and reactive case detection activities), there is opportunity to rigorously evaluate these various interventions.

Progress since PMI was launched

Results from a recently completed OR study that assessed seroprevalence in schools showed a wider prevalence range than microscopy for both *P. falciparum* (0-50% vs 0-12.7%) and *P. vivax* (0-53.7% and 0-4.5%), respectively. Overall, 11.6% (688/5,913) were *P. falciparum* seropositive and 11.1% (735/6,609) *P. vivax* seropositive; compared to 1.0% and 0.5% microscopy positive, respectively. Such studies could help determine transmission intensity within discrete communities in Ethiopia. PMI is also supporting an OR study to assess the utility of conducting serologic testing using previously collected dried blood spots from the 2011 MIS to provide information on collection of additional biomarkers in household surveys in settings where malaria transmission is very low and/or seasonal. Due to delays in procurement of the needed reagents, the laboratory testing is scheduled for summer of 2015.

The feasibility of using the dried tube specimen method for preserving *Plasmodium falciparum* parasites for use as QC samples for RDTs was assessed in 2013 and the results published in January 2015. The study noted that for all the time points evaluated, dried tube specimens stored at both the reference laboratory and health facility were reactive on RDTs stored under the recommended temperature and under field conditions, and the dried tube specimens without malaria parasites were negative. They concluded that the dried tube specimen method can be used under field conditions to supplement other RDT QC methods and assess health worker proficiency in Ethiopia and possibly other malaria-endemic countries.

Progress during the last 12-18 months

PMI recently supported an OR study performed at EPHI which analyzed the genotypic prevalence of G6PD deficiency among 1,585 dried blood spots obtained from the MIS 2011, The only G6PD deficient genotype detected was G6PD*A (A376G, 8.71%) with no samples positive for the clinically significant A- or Mediterranean variants, therefore suggesting a low expected frequency of drug-induced anemia from primaquine antimalarial therapy among Ethiopians.

Operational research activities supported with PMI FY 2015 funds include: 1) CQ weekly suppression of *P. vivax* infections among pregnant women (concept note development ongoing; pending approvals, field work is expected to begin in late 2015); 2) evaluation of single-dose primaquine therapy roll-out, assuming implementation of primaquine for first-line *P. falciparum* infections in elimination districts; and 3) evaluation of the roll-out of primaquine radical cure for *P. vivax* in hospital and health center settings.

PMI also provided core funding in 2015 for a multi-country OR activity that will assess safety aspects of the current iCCM protocols in malaria RDT-negative children with fever at rural health posts which is currently scheduled to begin mid-2015.

Table 12: PMI-funded operational research studies

Completed OR Studies			
Title	**Start date**	**End date**	**Budget**
G6PD variant survey	Jan 2014	March 2015	$90,000
School based seroprevalence	Oct 2011	Sept 2013	$200,000
Field assessment of dried tube specimens for RDT quality control and proficiency testing	Jan 2013	July 2013	$10,000
Ongoing OR Studies	**Start date**	**End date**	**Budget**
Title			
Malaria serology as a MIS biomarker	March 2014	Oct 2015	$70,000
Chloroquine prohylaxis for pregnant women with *P. vivax* pregnancy	March 2016	March 2017	$200,000
Evaluation of the roll out of single-dose primaquine for *P. falciparum*	Oct 2015	Sept 2017	$500,000
Evaluation of radical cure primaquine for *P. vivax*	Oct 2015	Oct 2016	$150,000
Planned OR Studies FY 2016			
Title	**Start date (est.)**	**End date (est.)**	**Budget**
Evaluation of reactive case detection and presumptive treatment of the index households	Oct 2016	Sept 2017	$400,000

Proposed activities with FY 2016 funding: **($410,000)**

- **Evaluation of reactive case detection and presumptive treatment of the index households ($400,000):** PMI will support the evaluation of FMOH's plans to conduct reactive case detection and presumptive treatment of index cases/households in designated malaria pre-elimination districts in order to inform malaria elimination strategies regarding case detection activities in Ethiopia to halt local transmission, clear up malaria transmission foci, and reduce the number of locally acquired cases to zero. The main purpose of this study is to assess a strategy of administering presumptive treatment of all household members of the index case due to the limited sensitivities of available diagnostic tools and evidence from other settings that additional infections were most often found in the index household. PMI will collect filter paper samples from the index households and their immediate neighbors (radius of <50-100m) to assess actual infection prevalence in these groups to help assess the strategy. As the elimination-specific interventions are still under discussion, PMI will closely consult with the FMOH in the design of this evaluation.
- **Technical assistance for OR ($10,000):** One TDY from CDC will be provided to support OR activities.

9. Staffing and administration

Two highly trained health professionals serve as resident advisors to oversee PMI's projects and activities in Ethiopia, one representing CDC and one representing USAID. In addition, four Foreign

Service Nationals (FSNs) work as part of the PMI team (two Senior Malaria Technical Advisors, one Malaria Advisor, and one Program Manager). All PMI staff members are part of a single interagency team led by the USAID Mission Director or his/her designee in Ethiopia. The PMI team shares responsibility for development and implementation of PMI strategies and work plans, coordination with national authorities, managing collaborating agencies and supervising day-to-day activities. Candidates for resident advisor positions (whether initial hires or replacements) will be evaluated and/or interviewed jointly by USAID and CDC, and both agencies will be involved in hiring decisions, with the final decision made by the individual agency.

The PMI professional staff work together to oversee all technical, programmatic and administrative aspects of the PMI, including finalizing details of the project design, implementing malaria prevention and treatment activities, monitoring and evaluation of outcomes and impact, reporting of results, and providing guidance to PMI partners.

The PMI lead in country is the USAID Mission Director. The day-to-day lead for PMI is delegated to the USAID Health Office Director and thus the two PMI resident advisors, one from USAID and one from CDC, report to the USAID Health Office Director for day-to-day leadership, and work together as a part of a single interagency team. The technical expertise housed in Atlanta and Washington guides PMI programmatic efforts.

The two PMI resident advisors are based within the USAID health office and are expected to spend approximately half their time sitting with and providing technical assistance to the national malaria control programs and partners.

Locally-hired staff to support PMI activities either in Ministries or in USAID will be approved by the USAID Mission Director. Because of the need to adhere to specific country policies and USAID accounting regulations, any transfer of PMI funds directly to Ministries or host governments will need to be approved by the USAID Mission Director and Controller, in addition to the US Global Malaria Coordinator.

Proposed activities with FY 2016 funding: **($2,050,000)**

- **CDC staffing ($450,000):** Salary support for one CDC Resident Advisor.

- **USAID staffing and management ($1,600,000):** Support to five staff members, including one USAID senior Resident Advisor and four FSNs based at the USAID Mission within the U.S. Embassy in Addis Ababa. The support includes all work-related expenses (e.g., salaries, benefits/ICASS, travel, supplies, etc.), and Mission-based expenditures, including USAID Mission expenses incurred in the direct implementation of PMI activities.

Table 1: Budget Breakdown by Mechanism

President's Malaria Initiative – Ethiopia
Planned Malaria Obligations for FY 2016

Mechanism	Geographic Area	Activity	Budget ($)	%
TBD – Supply Chain Contract	National	Procurement and distribution of LLINs, RDTs, laboratory equipment and supplies, chloroquine, primaquine, pre-referral and severe antimalarial drugs; support for national commodities' micro-planning	$17,676,000	44.2%
IRS 2 TO 6	Oromia/ National	IRS insecticide procurement; IRS operations; Entomological monitoring and capacity-building; and IRS national level technical assistance	$9,350,000	23.4%
CDC IAA	National	In-country staff; administrative expenses, TDYs, entomology supplies and equipment; and FELTP	$844,000	2.1%
SBCC- Health JHU-CCP	National	SBCC for LLINs, IRS, ACTs, and case management	$1,500,000	3.8%
APS-JU	Oromia	APS for local implementation of SBCC campaigns	$200,000	0.5%
APS-HDAMA	Amhara	APS for local implementation of SBCC campaigns	$200,000	0.5%
ICAP	Oromia/ National	Support for QA system for malaria laboratory diagnosis	$500,000	1.3%
TBD	Oromia/ National	Support for QA system for malaria laboratory diagnosis	$1,200,000	3.0%
TBD	National	Strengthening of drug management system capacity at regional, districts and health facilities	$1,000,000	2.5%
TBD	National	PFSA strengthening, coordination and reporting commodity status	$400,000	1.0%
USP PQM	National	Strengthen drug quality monitoring and support regulatory actions	$500,000	1.3%
TRANSFORM	National	Provide systems support for ongoing supervision, training and monitoring of malaria case management at health facility level	$1,900,000	4.8%
TBD	National	Private sector support to malaria prevention and control activities including development corridor areas.	$800,000	2.0%
SMMES	National	Support for malaria monitoring and evaluation, technical assistance and operational research	$1,800,000	4.5%
JHPIEGO-HRH	National	Expanding HEWs pre-service training	$300,000	0.8%
Peace Corps	National	PCVs malaria prevention activities	$30,000	0.1%
TBD	National	Capacity development of local NGOs for malaria prevention and control	$200,000	0.5%
USAID Staffing & Administration	National	Staffing and administration	$1,600,000	4.0%
Total			**$40,000,000**	**100%**

Table 2: Budget Breakdown by Activity
President's Malaria Initiative – Ethiopia
Planned Malaria Obligations for FY 2016

Proposed Activity	Mechanism	Budget		Geographic Area	Description
		Total $	Commodity $		
PREVENTIVE ACTIVITIES					
Insecticide-treated Nets					
LLIN procurement and distribution	TBD – Supply Chain Contract	$13,160,000	$13,160,000	National	Provide 4,000,000 free LLINs to district to distribute through health facilities, HEWs and other networks
LLIN distribution from districts to health posts	TBD – Supply Chain Contract	$600,000		National	LLIN distribution from districts to health posts
SUBTOTAL ITNs		$13,760,000	$13,160,000		
Indoor Residual Spraying					
IRS operations	IRS 2 TO 6	$8,500,000	$4,250,000	Oromia Region	Training, implementation and supervision support for IRS operations in 26 districts; procurement of spray equipment and PPE; procurement of insecticide for IRS activities and national level technical assistance

68

Activity	Mechanism	Amount		Location	Description
Entomological monitoring and capacity building	IRS 2 TO 6	$600,000		National	Expanding entomological monitoring for vector control and sustaining the capacity
National level technical assistance for vector control	IRS 2 TO 6	$250,000		National	Provide TA for curriculum development and conduct national level vector control training
Entomological supplies and equipment	CDC IAA	$10,000	$10,000	National	Provide critical supplies, reagents, and equipment for routine entomological monitoring activities and resistance and bionomic studies
Entomological technical assistance	CDC IAA	$29,000		National	Provide two TDYs from CDC/Atlanta for training, planning, and monitoring entomological activities
Molecular markers of insecticide resistance for *An. arabiensis*	CDC IAA	$75,000	$75,000	National	Provide supplies, reagents and equipment for molecular markers of insecticide resistance studies to EPHI and Ethiopian universities
SUBTOTAL IRS		$9,464,000	$4,335,000		
Malaria in Pregnancy					
Strengthening case management of MIP	TRANSFORM	$200,000		National	Support malaria case management of pregnant women in high transmission areas
Subtotal Malaria in Pregnancy		$200,000	$0		
SUBTOTAL PREVENTIVE		$23,224,000	$17,495,000		

CASE MANAGEMENT

Diagnosis and Treatment				
Procurement of RDTs	TBD – Supply Chain Contract	$1,884,000	$1,884,000	National	Procurement and distribution of 2,900,000 RDTs to support FMOH/ORHB efforts to scale-up RDT use at the health post level
Procurement of laboratory equipment/supplies	TBD – Supply Chain Contract	$400,000	$400,000	National	Procurement of laboratory equipment and supplies (e.g., microscopes), and including logistics systems support.
Support for QA system for malaria laboratory diagnosis	ICAP	$500,000		National	Support for refresher training, supervision, other QA/QC activities, and program monitoring; training and accreditation for laboratory supervisors
Support for QA system for malaria laboratory diagnosis	TBD	$1,200,000		National	Support for refresher training, supervision, other QA/QC activities, and program monitoring; training and accreditation for laboratory supervisors
Procurement of chloroquine and primaquine	TBD – Supply Chain Contract	$460,000	$460,000	National	Procurement of chloroquine and primaquine for national need.

Activity	Source	Budget	Budget	Location	Description
Procurement of pre-referral and severe malaria drugs	TBD – Supply Chain Contract	$822,000	$822,000	National	Procurement of pre-referral treatment and drugs for severe malaria
Provide support for ongoing supervision and monitoring of malaria diagnosis and treatment	TRANSFORM	$1,700,000		National	Support for health worker supervision, training and mentoring for management of malaria at health centers and health posts; collaboration with Zonal and District Health Offices
Private sector support to malaria prevention, control and case management	TBD	$800,000		Amhara & Oromia Regions	Work with the RHBs and private health facilities/farms/mining companies in Amhara and Oromia to increase access to quality malaria services
Subtotal Diagnosis and Treatment		$7,766,000	$3,556,000		
Pharmaceutical Management					
Strengthening of drug management system capacity	TBD	$1,000,000		National	Strengthening of drug management system, quantification and procurement; distribution management; and health facility drug availability

Activity	Mechanism	Location	Budget	Description
PFSA strengthening for reporting and management of malaria commodities	TBD	National	$400,000	Integrate malaria commodities into existing Integrated Pharmaceuticals Logistics System and improve management of malaria commodities quantification, drug exchange/transfer, and expiry tracking
Strengthen drug quality monitoring	USP PQM	National	$500,000	Support to FMHACA for monitoring post-market antimalarial drug quality, and building laboratory capacity at regional and national levels
Subtotal Pharmaceutical Management			$1,900,000	$0
SUBTOTAL CASE MANAGEMENT			$9,666,000	$3,566,000
HEALTH SYSTEM STRENGTHENING / CAPACITY BUILDING				
Coordination support for ORHB & NMCP	SMMES	National/ Oromia Region	$250,000	Support joint planning, coordination, supervision and review activities with all malaria stakeholders in ORHB/national level
Pre-service training of HEWs	JHPIEGO-HRH	National	$300,000	Pre-service training of HEWs to ensure that malaria will be focused in pre-service training for management of malaria at community level
Field Epidemiology & Laboratory Training Program	CDC IAA	National	$250,000	Support for applied epidemiology and laboratory training for three to five residents

Activity	Partner/Mechanism	Budget	Location	Description
Peace Corps malaria prevention activities	Peace Corps	$30,000	National	Support Peace Corps work on malaria at community level
Local NGO empowerment	TBD	$200,000	National	Capacity development of local NGOs for malaria prevention and control
SUBTOTAL HSS & CAPACITY BUILDING		$1,030,000	$0	
BEHAVIOR CHANGE COMMUNICATION				
Capacity building and coordination of SBCC activities for LLINs, IRS, ACTs, case management	SBCC-Health JHU-CCP	$450,000	National	National and regional level coordination, policy/guideline and tool review/development for malaria SBCC
Community-based SBCC for LLINs, IRS, ACTs, case management	SBCC-Health JHU-CCP	$1,050,000	National	Dissemination and implementation of various SBCC approaches through a variety of community platforms in high transmission areas
Community-based SBCC	APS-JU	$200,000	Oromia Region	Community-based SBCC through schools and FBOs for prevention and control of malaria in Oromia Region
Community-based SBCC	APS-HDAMA	$200,000	Amhara Region	Community-based SBCC through schools and FBOs for prevention and control of malaria in Amhara Region
SUBTOTAL SBCC		$1,900,000		

MONITORING AND EVALUATION				
Strengthening PHEM system and epidemic response	SMMES	$1,000,000	National	Strengthening the Public Health Emergency Management system; strengthen reporting of malaria cases from the health post to the health centers in hotspot districts to strengthen malaria epidemic detection and response
National malaria commodities micro-plan	TBD	$350,000	National	Support annual malaria commodity micro-planning
LLIN durability monitoring	SMMES	$150,000	National	Year 3 of LLIN durability monitoring
M&E technical assistance	CDC IAA	$20,000	National	Two TDYs to support M&E activities
SUBTOTAL M&E		$1,520,000		
OPERATIONS RESEARCH				
Evaluation of reactive case detection	SMMES	$400,000	National	Evaluation of FMOH's plans to conduct reactive case detection and presumptive treatment of the index households in selected elimination districts
OR Technical assistance- CDC TDY	CDC IAA	$10,000	National	One TDY to support new operational research
SUBTOTAL OR		$410,000		
IN-COUNTRY STAFFING AND ADMINISTRATION				

CDC Staffing and Management	CDC IAA	$450,000	National	Salaries, benefits of in-country CDC PMI staff (1)
USAID Staffing and Management	USAID	$1,600,000	National	Salaries and benefits of in-country USAID PMI staff (1 PSC and 4 FSNs); ICASS support of CDC PMI staff; administrative costs
SUBTOTAL IN-COUNTRY STAFFING		$2,050,000		
GRAND TOTAL		**$40,000,000**	**$21,061,000**	**Commodities (52.7 %)**

www.ingramcontent.com/pod-product-compliance
Lightning Source LLC
Chambersburg PA
CBHW081239280526

45787CB00006B/2721